中国国家汉办赠送
Donated by Hanban, China

Lifestyle in China

Gong Wen

translation by Li Ziliang, Zhao Feifei & Li Zhaoguo

CHINA
INTERCONTINENTAL
PRESS

JOURNEY INTO CHINA

Counsellor: Cai Wu
General Director: Li Bing
Chief Editors: Guo Changjian & Li Xiangping
Deputy Chief Editor: Wu Wei

图书在版编目（CIP）数据

生活之旅：英文／龚纹著；李子亮，赵菲菲，李照国译.
—北京：五洲传播出版社，2007.8（2008.5重印）
（中国之旅）
ISBN 978-7-5085-1102-3

I．生…
II．①龚… ②李… ③赵… ④李…
III．社会生活－概况－中国－英文
IV．D669

中国版本图书馆CIP数据核字（2007）第064529号

LIFESTYLE IN CHINA

Author: Gong Wen
Translator: Li Ziliang, Zhao Feifei & Li Zhaoguo
Planner: Feng Lingyu
Project Director: Deng Jinhui
Executive Editor: Qin Tiantian
Art Director: Tian Lin
Photo Credit: Imagine China, China Foto Press,
    Hong Kong *China Tourism*, FOTOE, Quan Jing Photo
Publisher: China Intercontinental Press (6 Beixiaomachang, Lianhuachi
    Donglu, Haidian District, Beijing 100038, China)
Printer: Beijing Picture in Picture Printing Co., Ltd.
Tel: 86-10-58891281
Website: www.cicc.org.cn
Edition: Aug. 2007, 1st edition, May. 2008, 2nd print run
Format: 787×1092mm 1/16
Signatures: 11
Words: 53,000
Print Run: 7001–14,000
Price: RMB 98.00 (yuan)

CONTENTS

THE REAL LIVES OF THE CHINESE PEOPLE

Twenty years ago, foreign tourists from other countries learned about China through such wonders as "The Great Wall," "The Forbidden City" and "pandas." Since then, the keywords about China have reached such a high number that they can no longer be measured in digits. The present tourism environment, which is open to the outside world, and the Internet has continually helped to present a more real China than it used to be reported in the mass media. Though characterized by the magnitude of time, China, like an old friend, will surely evoke a warm response. Learning about China does not mean simply looking up to the big and great country as she is presented; what's more important is feeling the charms she infuses in the real lives of the Chinese people. Only through close contact in their actual lives can a realistic understanding of China and her people be gained.

As China is a big, traditional, agricultural country, grain has always been sacrosanct. The Chinese people not only value food greatly from the bottom of their hearts, they are familiar with the how's and why's of food as well as its appeal. Various wonderful methods of cooking and the commonly used seasonings together lead to the five tastes of sour, sweet, bitter, pungent and salty and result in the singular sight of Oriental food, which comprises color, fragrance, taste, meaning, form and nutrition. Delicious food embraces not only a revelry of tastes, but is also the most extensive and profound folk culture that is rooted in the lives of average people, just as the magical appeal of roast duck lies not only in the dish, but also in the process of

its being precisely sliced, just as the deliciousness of the chafing-dish lies not only on the tips of our tongues, but also in all the tempting aromas wafting from a chafing-dish. Celebrations on festive occasions are also underscored with food. From Spring Festival (Chinese New Year) to the Laba Festival (the eighth day of the twelfth lunar month), all festival-related food, ranging from *jiaozi*, New Year Cakes to sticky rice dumplings and *zongzi*, makes the traditional Chinese festivals more lively and interesting. Chinese food culture is extensive and profound. From light breakfasts along the streets to the hundreds of local dishes, including an array of dishes of the Manchu and Han nationalities, regardless of the complexity or simplicity of the processes through which they are made, they all contribute to the enrichment of the lives of the Chinese.

The Chinese discovered and manufactured tea, and tea instills the tranquil and refined temperament into the Chinese nation. Tea plucking, tea manufacturing and tea drinking form the essence of traditional Chinese culture. Tea set, tea etiquette and tea ceremony brilliantly reflect the Chinese aesthetics of life. Sitting in a courtyard and drinking a bowl of jasmine tea in spring will offer the heart a pleasurable trip around the ancient capital of Beijing. If you happen to be in a teahouse in south

China in summer, whether it's noisy or quiet, a cup of mild, pure Kung Fu Oolong Tea will refresh and comfort you as it slides down your throat. In autumn, how pleasant to taste strong, mellow, traditional *pu'er* tea while travelling along ancient roads! In winter, when a group of good friends gather around a stove in a Mongolian yurt, drinking mare's milk and brick tea, they will be transported, body and soul, with its salty aroma and warmth. The spirit of tea drinking, which bolsters nature and is free and unconstrained, has continued throughout the ages and still has a great effect on the Chinese people.

If the consensus is that "people regard food as their primary requirement," wine can be thought of as the timely rains bestowed by the heavens. Deeply immersed in the fragrance of wine, the Chinese nation has followed the wine-brewing concept that "wine is the crystallization of grains" for over 1,000 years. Wine culture traces its history back to ancient times. In ancient China, wine was closely associated with religion, politics and military affairs. In addition, wine played an even more significant role in the cultural lives of people. Learned men of all ages forged an unbreakable connection with wine. Shaoxing wine, which tastes mild and mellow, has till now been exclusive to China. *Moutai* wine, the national wine of China and also one of the three major distilled wines in the world, has long been regarded as China's heavily fragrant calling card. For the Chinese people, drinking wine is a crucial way of life. More important, it is also a way of entertaining and socializing. Vintage wine and the protocol, good habits and customs in wine drinking comprise the Chinese wine culture, which conveys warm, genuine feelings while simultaneously revealing the Chinese mindset that a feast is incomplete without wine, is not proper without wine and is not considered a celebration without wine.

Leisure-time entertainment of the Chinese people is also multifold. Today, you may go to Liulichang of Beijing to search for ancient classics, works of calligraphy, paintings and seals. You may also choose a random street corner and join any one of the groups of elderly chess players. Various traditional Chinese operas are staged in opera houses, while folk artists tell stories or sing ballads about the lives of average people on the fairs on street corners. The relaxed ambiance deserves being savored and considered. The Chinese firmly uphold the belief of the perfect unity of heaven, people and *qi*, and this in turn results in the principles of maintaining good health—that people should behave in accordance with the laws of nature. To achieve good health and sound mind by following the will of heaven is the Chinese people's philosophy of life, as is taking care of one's self in order to enjoy the course of one's natural life.

Now, Chinese food is ready to challenge your bold appetite. Top-quality tea and mellow wine will take you to the Orient of which you have been dreaming. The games of intelligence, which have been the gratification of several thousand years, will arouse you from your deep sleep. And the Chinese way of keeping fit will unfold its philosophy so that you may take good care of your health. Here, we've included all these aspects of the lives of the Chinese people and hope you can enjoy them to the fullest.

Yang Ping

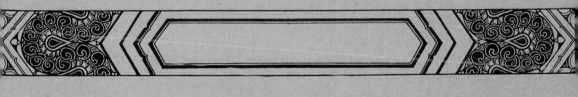

PARADISE FOR FOOD LOVERS

Enjoying Foods in Chinese Festivals

Nowadays, if you casually leaf through any Chinese calendar, you'll notice that many days among the 365 days of one year are gaily noted with festive occasions and commemorations. Undoubtedly, the festival-related food with unique Chinese characteristics plays a significant part in the celebration of the traditional Chinese festivals and holidays.

Spring Festival marks the beginning of the Chinese New Year, according to the Chinese lunar calendar. Also, it is the most important festival for the Chinese people.

A saying among northern Chinese people goes, "No-one wouldn't love to have a bowl of *jiaozi* for the New Year." But southern Chinese people do not subscribe to this belief. Actually, the "New Year food" shared by all the Chinese people from both the north and south is "New Year cake" (*nian gao*), which literally can be interpreted as "The quality of life is improving year by year." The

Food is indispensable to every Chinese festive celebration.

Yuanxiao. The gist of traditional Chinese culture has been handed down to us through the rich and colorful festival-related Chinese food.

New Year cakes from the north, which are mostly sweet, is either steamed or deep-fried. The New Year cakes with hundreds of fruits are a traditional specialty snack popular in Beijing. The northeastern people make New Year cakes with sticky, husked *kaoliang* flour. People from Shanxi Province love to eat New Year cakes made of sticky millet flour, while people from Hebei Province love to add dates and mung-bean flour in their New Year cake recipe. Aside from steaming and deep-frying, New Year cakes popular in south China can also be fried and cooked with both salty and sweet flavors. New Year cakes in Jiangsu and Zhejiang provinces, which are light, are made of round-grained, non-sticky rice flour and are good to fry and cook. Preserved ham, dried shrimp and mushrooms picked in winter are added to the radish

It is a time-honored tradition to eat *zongzi* at the Dragon Boat Festival.

cakes and taro cakes popular in Guangdong Province; these cakes have a typical flavor, and are deliciously refreshing. New Year cakes were usually hand-made in the past. In the south this is called "husking rice with mortar and pestle to make New Year cakes," which is regarded as a grand occasion among peasant families there.

First of all, husked rice, which has been soaked in water for a couple of days, is milled into thick liquid on the millstone, drip-dried and then steamed in an iron cooker. After it is steamed, the whole family, old and young, all pitch in and pour it into a stone mortar. The very young, while singing, pound the rice flour with big, wooden pestles, and the old and older children add water and turn over the rice flour, thus ushering in the New Year in the lively activity of husking rice with mortar and pestle to make New Year cakes.

As the saying goes, "Spring Festival won't be over until the 15th day of the first lunar month" and the celebration lasts as long, and the last day of this

For the Chinese people, moon cakes are a must to go with the Mid-Autumn Festival.

celebration falls on another major traditional folk festival, the Lantern Festival (*Yuanxiao Jie*). Naturally, the Chinese eat rice dumplings (*yuanxiao*) at this festival. People from the north call rice dumplings *yuanxiao*, while people from the south call them *tangyuan*. Both *yuanxiao* and *tangyuan* are made of sticky rice flour and filling and are round, signifying "union and togetherness." When making *yuanxiao*, the northerners first mix sesame, peanuts, sweet bean paste and other ingredients, forming small pieces, then placing them into large bamboo or wicker baskets that contain rice flour. They rock the baskets and sprinkle water continuously on the rice flour in order to make the filling and rice flour form full, round balls. Southerners make *tangyuan* by wrapping the filling with the sticky rice flour wrapping and then crumpling them into balls. *Tangyuan* is usually larger than *yuanxiao* and its filling can be sweet or salty. Southerners also use green vegetables as filling to make large, delectable and lovely *tangyuan*. Just a couple of *tangyuan* are enough for a meal.

During the Dragon Boat Festival, which arrives in early summer and lands on the fifth day of the fifth lunar month, all families fully participate in picking bamboo or reed leaves, washing sticky rice and wrapping *zongzi*. Two or three bamboo or reed leaves are placed on top of each other, creating a pyramid; sticky rice and filling are poured into it and cotton thread is wrapped around this. Boiled *zongzi* is exquisite and satisfying. If you have *zongzi* with white sugar or honey, you'll be struck by its pleasantly sweet flavor. The filling of the *zongzi* as prepared by the northerners is sweet, chiefly consisting of small dates and sweetened bean paste. The *zongzi* made by southerners also contains salty fillings, such as meat, ham and yolk, which contrasts nicely with the sweet, aromatic sticky rice.

In autumn, the Mid-Autumn Festival, the second most important traditional festival for the Chinese people, arrives with the full moon. The mid-autumn moon cakes echo the shape of the full moon, symbolizing "union and togetherness." On the night of the Mid-Autumn Festival, all families gather to appreciate the bright, full moon and eat moon cakes. How happy and close each family is when they gather to enjoy the bright, full moon! Various flavors can be savored, including Beijing-Flavored, Guangdong-Flavored, Suzhou-Flavored, Yunnan-Flavored, Chaozhou-Flavored, Hong-Kong-Flavored, etc. Among these, Guangdong-Flavored is the most popular among the Chinese. Shiny and smooth, these cakes have a thin skin and rich stuffing. Apart from traditional stuffing such as the five nuts, sweet bean paste, lotus seed mash and yolk, almost anything that is edible can be made into stuffing of Guangdong-Flavored moon cakes. Do not be surprised if you come across moon cakes with a champagne or cheese flavor on Mid-Autumn Festival.

As an essential part of life, food is present every day from the beginning of the year to the end of the year, when winter arrives quickly. Laba Festival, which falls on the eighth day of the 12th lunar month, is the prelude to Spring Festival. On this day, families throughout China put all kinds of food grains into their cookers and make Laba porridge. The food grains boiled in today's Laba porridge number more than eight and the porridge, made with cereals, beans, potatoes, nuts, dried and candied fruits and vegetables, is both delicious and healthful. Also on this day, people from the north put new garlic in matured vinegar and preserve it till New Year's Eve, when, along with Laba garlic and Laba vinegar to accompany *jiaozi*, they enjoy their first dinner of the coming New Year with great gusto.

All the Tempting Aromas from One Chafing Dish

The history of the Chinese people's eating hotpot dishes can be traced back 10,000 years. The *ding* (an ancient pot with two round handles and three or four legs), which today can be seen in museums, is actually the beginning of ancient hotpots. However, hotpots specifically used for cooking food were reportedly invented by the descendants of Genghis Khan. The Mongolians loved to eat mutton but when troops were on a march or during war, cooking large pieces of mutton was too time-consuming, so the soldiers cut frozen mutton into thin slices, dipped and cooked them in boiling water, then retrieved them

Food suitable for chafing dish is so rich and varied that it may well meet the requirement that meat and vegetables should complement each other to make a balanced diet.

instantly and spread on refined salt before devouring them. Prepared this way, mutton tasted fresh and tender and could be cooked very quickly. This can be regarded as the beginning of the hotpot mutton dish.

Nowadays, the hotpot mutton dish still occupies a crucial role in the family of hotpot dishes. *Donglaishun*, a long-established restaurant noted for its hotpot grassland mutton in Beijing, has a history of 100 years in using traditional charcoal fire and a copper pot. As thin as cicada wings, each mutton slice is no wider than 1 mm and is cooked instantly once dipped in the hotpot. However, the mutton can never be overdone even if boiled for a long time. Moreover, the fat is not greasy and the meat is not dry. Light soup is usually the most popular for traditional dipped mutton, but there are as many as a dozen seasonings to complement the mutton, including sesame paste, soy sauce, rice vinegar, Shaoxing wine, thick chili oil, shrimp oil, fermented bean curd, chive flowers, sweetened garlic, coriander and chopped green onion.

Echoing this mutton dish in the far north is the hot and spicy chafing dish in and around south Chongqing. "Hot" is exclusive to the Chongqing chafing dish; with many red hot peppers, the Chongqing chafing dish is hot, spicy and delicious. After this dish was introduced to other parts of China, the customers who were not used to hot dishes were also tempted to try it. As a result, the mandarin-duck chafing dish, which resembles the *Taiji* symbol, came into being, with light soup and hot soup being separated from each other, so customers could choose whichever they preferred.

Apart from the two places of origin of the chafing dish, one from the north and the other from the south, the chafing dish has become extremely popular throughout China. The soup for the chafing dish can be light, hot and spicy, of various delicacies, sour and hot, and even act as a tonic. The food contained in the chafing dish includes almost anything edible, from birds and beasts to fish as well as seasonal vegetables. The seasonings can be

Traditional charcoal hot pot. Beef and mutton done in such pots taste most delicious.

sesame paste, sesame oil, hot peppers, onion, garlic and vinegar. The chafing dish includes a medley of endless varieties of all food and an infinite possibility of all tastes. In the beginning, people had chafing dishes only in the winter to warm themselves. But today, many people also love to have them with iced beer in air-conditioned rooms on sultry summer days.

When talking about the dish, the world-famous Chinese tableware, chinaware and chopsticks must be included in the conversation. The mutton slices from *Donglaishun* are as thin as silk. When placed on a blue-and-white porcelain plate, the floral designs are distinctly visible. For this reason, blue-and-white porcelain plates have become the standard in discriminating mutton, which has contributed a significant element to the *Donglaishun* chafing dish culture. China plates and china bowls are not only an aspect of this culture, but also

Nowadays, chopsticks can not only serve as daily tableware, they can also be used as gifts and handicraft articles, and they even have become "luxury items."

the principal tableware on dinner tables in China. The chinaware, which has gone through countless processes in its production from start to finish, such as choice of material, base-making, drying, glazing, burning and so on, is free from sediment and grime. It is indeed the best home for food. And a pair of chopsticks, consisting of two thin, long bamboo sticks, the top being thicker and square and the bottom being thinner and round, are the best and necessary tools for eating. The form makes the sticks easy to grasp and the food easy to eat. Chopsticks make it easy to take almost everything from the chafing dish, prevent the hands from getting burned and are more sanitary.

Roast Duck—The Calling Card of Beijing Food

In Beijing, hosts usually opt for roast duck as their first choice when entertaining friends from afar, and there are almost no exceptions to this rule. Beijing roast duck has simply become the calling card of Beijing food.

Eating roast duck provides the revelry of tastes, as well as a visual pleasure. Slicing the duck is worthy of being described as a superb, artistic and precisely calculated performance. The bright, clean, jade-like slices, along with the gold, translucent skin, fall onto the plate one after another as the thin knife-edge moves swiftly. A duck is usually sliced in 80 to 100 pieces and the cuts weigh about 0.6 kg. The bones are returned to the kitchen and cooked over a big fire; almost instantly, a bowl of delicious, milky duck soup will be taken to the dinner table.

There are many ways to eat roast duck. But the most common food and vegetables to accompany roast duck are a combination of thin pancakes, sweet sauce made of fermented flour, shredded scallion and long, narrow pieces of cucumber. First, sweet sauce is spread on a thin pancake, then roast duck, shredded scallion and cucumber are added, and finally "sandwiched" together gently. In this small "package" is the whole spectrum of Chinese food staples: meat, vegetables, garnishes

A plague of Beijing Roast Duck Restaurant, a restaurant of long standing in Dashilan, Beijing.

Upper: *Gualu* Roast Duck.
Beijing roast duck which is famous both at home and abroad.

Lower: Slicing roast duck.

Quanjude Roast Duck Restaurant filled with customers. *Quanjude* Roast Duck Restaurant was founded in 1864

and condiments. The nutrition of this small package is surprisingly well-balanced, not to mention delicious. The crispy skin can also be eaten with white sugar. The combined flavor of the meat and the cool sweetness is indescribable.

Generally, roast duck is made in two different ways: one is *gualu* roast duck (the duck is hung and roasted in an open stove) and the other is *menlu* roast duck (the duck is roasted in an enclosed stove). The *Quanjude gualu* roast duck is renowned both at home and abroad and the *Bianyifang menlu* roast duck has a long history. *Gualu* roast duck is made over a roaring fire on an open stove, and fruit trees are used as firewood. The skin is crispy and smoky with the fragrance of fruit trees. *Menlu* roast duck is roasted over the heat of burned sorghum and the oven door is closed tightly. Each method has its own merit, but, either way, the duck are both famous for their crispy skin, tender meat and are equally perfect and delicious.

Chinese Dumplings (*Jiaozi*)—The Most Delicious of All Food

The Chinese people's affection for Chinese dumplings (*jiaozi*) cannot be described with words, so they simply sum up: "Chinese dumplings are the most delicious of all food."

It is circulated among the people that *jiaozi* was invented by Zhang Zhongjing, the "Medicine Saint" during the last years of the Eastern Han Dynasty (25–220). Reportedly, Zhang Zhongjing noticed that many people's ears were frostbitten when he returned to his hometown one winter. He chopped up hot food such as mutton and rolled them up into ear-shaped forms with wheat flour wrappings using both hands. After boiling the ear-shaped food, he distributed it with boiled water to his fellow villagers. After the villagers, who were suffering with frostbitten ears, had eaten this preparation from the day of Winter Solstice to New Year's Eve, they

Chinese dumplings are like shoe-shaped ingots.

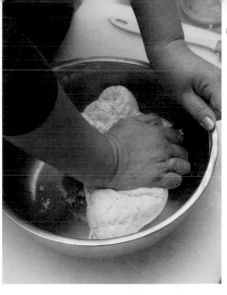

The process of making Chinese dumplings: making dough → making stuffing → rolling out dumpling wrappers → wrapping.

had fully recovered from their illness. In the beginning, people called this food *jiao'er*, and later the name *jiao'er* slowly became *jiaozi*.

Today, *jiaozi* is still a must for Spring Festival in most parts of north China, and making *jiaozi* a very important part of celebrating New Year's Eve for every family. The whole family, after washing their hands, sit in around the table and roll up their sleeves, wrapping up all their expectations for the coming new year in ear-shaped *jiaozi*, all the while chatting and laughing. Some families still observe the age-old custom of randomly putting a candy, a peanut and a coin into the *jiaozi*. It is said that whoever eats the *jiaozi* with the candy will lead a happy life in the

coming new year, whoever eats the *jiaozi* with the peanut will have good wealth and a long life, and whoever eats the *jiaozi* with the coin will be lucky in money matters.

The *jiaozi* filling is usually a mixture of meat and vegetables and the manner of eating *jiaozi* have few differences; vinegar is the basic sauce used to accompany *jiaozi*. The northerners prefer to have Laba vinegar and Laba garlic during Spring Festival. When eating *jiaozi*, drinkers also love to have a cup of liquor, which best illustrates the saying, "If one has *jiaozi* to go with liquor, the more he drinks, the more well-off he will be."

Nowadays, having already broken down traditional barriers, *jiaozi* filling can also include mountain delicacies and seafood delights, as well as seasonal and dried food. *Jiaozi* can be steamed, boiled, fried or deep-fried or baked, and it can be salty, sweet, hot or sour and can be made into shapes so exquisite, such as butterflies, goldfish, Chinese mandarin ducks and rabbits, that people do not have the heart to eat them.

To understand Chinese food, first try to make *jiaozi* yourself.

A prospering *jiaozi* restaurant. Traditionally, people in north China eat *jiaozi* on Winter Solstice, the 22nd or 23rd of December.

All Kinds of Noodles across China

Actually, China does not have the exclusive right to claim the invention of noodles. The Chinese and Italians were stalemated in this regard for years. It is said that actual noodles made 4,000 years ago were unearthed in Qinghai Province not long ago and this apparently has ended the disagreement. However, in fact, noodles are an internationally popular food and every nation has its own way of preparing and cooking noodles. In China alone there are over thousands of ways.

Beijing noodles served with fried-meat-sauce are the basic, common food for the daily consumption of Beijing people. This sauce is made by mixing soy bean sauce and

Noodles served with fried bean sauce of Old Beijing.

stir-fried diced, streaky pork, scallion, ginger and garlic. Seasonal vegetables are added, such as bean sprouts in early spring, tender leaves of Chinese toon in late spring, and new garlic and hyacinth beans in early summer. Today, restaurants specializing in this dish have retained the tradition of employing only waiters

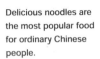

Delicious noodles are the most popular food for ordinary Chinese people.

to serve the customers. All the waiters wear Chinese-style uniforms and cloth shoes with soles of many cloth layers stitched together. They call and shout in Beijing dialect at the top of their lungs when greeting or saying goodbye to the customers, who must prepare themselves for the loud volume.

Most people think that noodles made by southerners are less satisfying than those made by northerners. However, Sichuan noodles with peppery sauce and Hubei noodles made of soda flour have won the goodwill of many people for their unique flavors. Similar to all Sichuan delicacies, Sichuan noodles with peppery sauce are known for their hotness. A spoonful of fried, savory, crisp minced meat is added to boiled hand-pulled noodles. Soup is made of sesame paste, pepper oil, seed powder of prickly Chinese ash, chopped green onion, minced garlic, eastern Sichuan vegetables, pea sprouts and other ingredients, and this mixture is poured onto the noodles. Such noodles taste spicy and hot. Hubei noodles are made of soda flour. When the noodles are boiled, oil is added and the noodles sit for a while to cool. Then they are boiled again, taken out of the pot, allowing the water to trickle off. Finally, minced dried radish, sesame paste and other seasonings are added; the noodles are shiny, smooth, chewy and tasty.

Hand-pulled noodles.

However, the people from the northwest are the best at making noodles. Qishan noodles with minced or diced meat are made as thin as cicada wings. The minced pork is cooked along with pepper and vinegar. Bean curd, dry lily and edible black fungus are usually used as garnish. Qishan noodles stress more oil, hot noodle soup and fewer noodles, which will make the noodles sour, hot and delicious. Xi'an noodles are wide and sprinkled with oil. The boiled noodles are placed into a bowl, minced scallion and meat are added, a thick layer of pepper powder is spread on, a spoonful of boiling peanut oil is poured into the bowl; instantly, the aroma of peppers waft through the air. When eating Lanzhou hand-pulled beef noodles, observe the cook, as pulling the noodles up and down is a graceful sight to behold. Dough can be pulled into various widths—as wide as Chinese chives

Shanxi cooks whittling off the dough into the boiling pot.

and as thin as a strand of hair. The broth for the noodles is made by cooking the beef, marrow, liver and bones with over a dozen spices. The soup is complete—mellow and savory. A gourmet's good fortune of enjoying the process of making noodles should be given equal emphasis with eating noodles cooked by whittling the dough into the boiling pot, which is popular in Shanxi Province. Standing near the pot of boiling water, the cook holds a piece of dough with his left hand and a tile-shaped knife with his right. As the cook whittles the dough, triangular noodles fall into the pot like snowflakes. Some master cooks even put the dough on their heads and whittle off the dough with both hands, dazzling all viewers with such a sight.

The Chinese people prefer to have noodles on birthdays, for noodles are usually long, thus carrying the message of longevity. The "one single noodle" popular in Shanxi Province gives full expression to the wishes for longevity—just one noodle can fill a bowl. This single noodle of one width can be as long as 20 meters. Therefore, when touring Shanxi some day, do not miss the long "one single noodle" even though it may not be your birthday.

The Magic of Stuffed Steamed Buns

A humorous story circulates about the origin of pizza: Marco Polo took a liking to Chinese meat pie after a trip to China. Among his friends was a cook from Naples, who tried to make a delicious Chinese meat pie for him, but was troubled over not knowing how to add the meat stuffing to the flour cake. Finally, he spread the meat stuffing onto the cake. Beyond expectations, the cake with meat stuffing was incredibly delicious. So, this was the first pizza ever made.

Actually, adding the meat stuffing is no secret. If the cook had known that the Chinese had gravy or soup wrapped in the stuffed steamed buns, he would have been even more stunned.

Stuffed steamed buns filled with minced meat and gravy or soup are very popular both in the north and south. The wrappings of such buns glisten and are

The newly-cooked steamed stuffed buns are like pure white lotus flowers.

translucent; not a single drop of gravy or soup will escape the wrapping. In Xi'an, Shaanxi Province, "Jia's Steamed Stuffed Buns Filled with Minced Meat and Gravy" has a nationwide reputation, and in Shanghai the "Nanxiang Steamed Stuffed Buns" is also renowned. "Stuffed Steamed Buns Filled with Meat and Gravy" are also local delicacies of Tianjin, Kaifeng City of Henan Province, Nanjing, Yangzhou and Jingjiang of Jiangsu Province.

As a matter of fact, the gravy or soup in the stuffed steamed buns takes shape not by being poured into the buns until they are well-cooked. The beauty of the gravy lies in the stuffing. The frequently used method is to cut pork skin into thin slices and cook them in meat-stock soup over a low fire. The skin and soup turn into jelly when cooled. This is the secret of making stuffed steamed buns filled with meat and gravy. As stuffing, the pork skin jelly is solid, but turns into gravy when heated. In the south, crab eggs and digestive parts are usually added. The imagination can run wild as regards how delicious such gravy can be. The Jia's Steamed Stuffed Buns popular in the north are also enjoyed by Muslims so, naturally, pork skin jelly cannot used. However, the Muslims, who are also fond of stuffed steamed buns, are not outwitted by this detail. They mix cattle and sheep bone soup with beef as stuffing, and gravy is made when the stuffing is warmed. The Muslims' stuffed steamed buns are equally delicious.

Steamed buns, which are various in kind, are one of the staple food the Chinese people prefer to eat. Vegetable and meat fillings are wrapped up with leavened dough wrappers.

Steamers made of
bamboo or wood.

People are enjoying the steaming steamed stuffed buns.

As each bun has over 30 furrows on its jade-like flour, a basket of just-made buns look like white chrysanthemums in full bloom. When held gently with chopsticks and lifted slowly, the "chrysanthemum blossom" transforms into a "lantern." The gravy, quivering slightly and visible through the thin, fragile wrapping, is dimly visible. Nevertheless, a novice will certainly make a spectacle of himself if he is too eager to bite such a wonderful delicacy. If caught off guard, he might be scalded or the people nearby might be splashed with gravy. When eating these buns, first take a small bite and then suck the gravy slowly. Eating the buns can be summed up: "Lift the buns gently and move them with caution; take a small bite first before drinking the gravy." In Chenghuangmiao, Shanghai, considerate restaurants even have straws for customers. There, many loyal fans of these buns can be found gazing fondly at the bun as they suck the gravy through the straw, like children. Instantly, contented smiles light up their faces.

Enjoying Breakfast—The First Meal of the Day

As a Chinese saying goes, "The whole year's work depends on a good start in spring, while a day's opportunities depend on the dawn." Of the three meals in a day, breakfast is the first meal upon awakening and has been much valued by all people throughout the ages.

Breakfast in different regions varies greatly both in content and form. Moreover, the customs of having breakfast are poles apart, too. Nevertheless, two kinds of food—soybean milk and deep-fried dough twists—accompany each other all the time. Soybean milk, either salty or sweet, is the traditional daily food of the Chinese people. Having warm soybean milk to go with fresh, golden, deep-fried dough twists, one solid and the other liquid, is indeed a treat. They are both simple and delicious.

Soya-bean milk and deep-fried twisted dough sticks are usually the most popular food for breakfast among Chinese people.

Jellied bean curd can be found almost everywhere in the country. The pure, white jellied bean curd is fine

and smooth, congealed but not solid, tender but not too slack. The condiments served in Beijing jellied bean curd include soy sauce bean curd juice, shrimp sauce, Chinese chive blossoms, sesame paste and pepper oil. The thick gravy that goes with this bean curd is braised with mushrooms and pork slices. The condiments that are served in the bean curd special to Qianxian County, Shaanxi Province, comprise ginger, minced garlic, soy sauce, five-flavored vinegar and ground pepper oil, which combined make the bean curd pungently delicious. In Suzhou jellied bean curd over a dozen condiments are added, such as dried shrimp, laver, kelp, pickled mustard slices, pepper paste, and, finally, shredded onion and sesame oil. Watching the process of making Suzhou jellied bean curd alone is also a treat. Dumpling soup (also known as *wonton*), made with thinner wrappings and lesser but more exquisite stuffing, is the variation of *jiaozi*, yet it is irregularly shaped and smaller. Both *jiaozi* and dumpling soup are equally delicious. Dumpling soup is known as *wonton* in Guangdong, *bianshi* in Fujian, *chaoshou* in Sichuan and *qingtang* in Jiangxi. Dumpling soup can be seen on breakfast tables everywhere in China. *Douzhi*, formally known as fermented drink made from water used in grinding green beans, appears light green and tastes sour and bitter. But the elderly people from Beijing love it, and will eat it with greater relish when they eat it with crispy, fried dough rings. *Chaogan*, too, is a traditional light Beijing breakfast. It is a thick and remarkable stew made of pig liver, intestines, yellow bean paste, broth, Chinese onion, minced ginger and garlic and starch. On early Beijing mornings, the elderly can always be seen holding bird cages and looking for *douzhi*, and taxi drivers can also be seen, chatting about international affairs while enjoying their *chaogan*.

Fried Chinese dough and egg filling wrapped and rolled in the thin, green bean flour pancake is a contribution to breakfast from the Tianjin people. Northern people call deep-fried dough twists "fried Chinese doughnuts." A spoonful of green bean flour paste

A young lady who has just bought her food for breakfast from the street.

is spread onto a flat-bottomed pan, an egg is added and this mixture is evened out; chopped onions are spread over this and the pancake is turned upside down quickly. Then a coating of sweet sauce made of fermented flour and chili paste is applied. Chopped coriander and sesame is spread on and a fried Chinese doughnut is placed on it, wrapped and rolled. It is done. A nice day starts with such a warm, delicious food as breakfast.

Going south leads to Yangzhou along the Yangtze River, where people have more leisurely breakfasts. All family members pick a teahouse along an aged lane, sit in a circle at a table, make a pot of green tea produced in the Taihu Lake area and order a dish of cooked, shredded

A breakfast stand selling thin pancakes.

bean curd and seven to eight baskets of delicacies. Steamed dumplings and stuffed steamed buns send forth a fragrant aroma; steamed dumplings with "shepherd's purse" stuffing with the dough trimmed at the top are green and translucent, and the wrappings of the steamed stuffed buns filled with the gravy of crab eggs and digestive parts are thin and delicate. The family enjoys the delicacies, along with vinegar, minced ginger and the cooked, shredded bean curd with fragrant tea, discussing the past and present in leisurely fashion.

Going further south leads to Guangdong, where breakfast lasts a much longer time, becomes a way to appreciate leisure and embraces having drink and food,

Guangdong style refreshments are ingenuously made. They are usually done through steaming and thus the original flavor of the foodstuff is well preserved.

as well as entertainment. In Guangdong, people call breakfast "morning tea," and drinking tea is also called "enjoying tea." Morning tea in Guangdong is indeed considered a treat. Morning tea begins at 4 a.m. and lasts till noon. Teahouses are packed during this time. On holidays, teahouse *aficionados* have to line in queues and wait for seats. Morning tea includes not only tea but also different porridges, dishes, steamed food and other treats. The types of porridge include purple millet, millet with a fragrant flavor, millet with preserved duck egg, and with fish slices. All this porridge can be either salty or sweet according to the customers' desires. The dishes include chicken feet, chewy beef and pork ribs. The small, stuffed steamed buns in the bamboo steamer taste delicious and not at all oily. Steamed dishes also include transparent dumplings with shrimp filling, and delicate dishes include gold egg-shaped buns. Meat steamed with rice flour consists of skewer-roasted pork, beef, fish-meat slices, shrimp, as well as soy sauce and fermented salty soybeans. Sticky rice with chicken is wrapped with lotus leaves. When it is unrolled, customers are greeted with the aroma of the sticky rice and the salty freshness of the chicken. It's hard not to be carried away by these delicacies, accompanied by a cup of oolong tea—during a family reunion, meeting friends, reading newspapers, chatting or just meditating.

Crab Specialties Will Be Served at Dinner
When Autumn Winds Rise

A saying in China goes: "Crab specialties will be served at dinner when autumn winds rise."

Eating crabs is not only a seasonal activity, the breeds and the regions can also determine their quality. Crabs are subdivided into freshwater crabs and sea crabs. The meat of freshwater crabs is tender and more delicious than sea crabs. Of all the freshwater crabs, *Dazha* crabs are the best, and the *Dazha* crabs produced in Yangcheng Lake, Suzhou, are regarded as authentic. *Dazha* crabs from Yangcheng Lake are plump and delicious, it is said, because the bottom of Yangcheng Lake is hard and the crabs develop their strong bodies and powerful legs by

Yangcheng Lake has a vast expanse of top quality water. Fences served for raising crabs can be seen everywhere on the lake.

walking on such a hard surface. Apart from being larger, *Dazha* crabs from Yangcheng Lake have special features of their own—"glistening green back, white belly, golden claws with yellowish hair." Nowadays, almost all the *Dazha* crabs from other regions can appear to be "green on the back and white on the belly" after people wash them. However, the golden fine hair on crab claws is still a point of pride and is exclusive to *Dazha* crabs from Yangcheng Lake.

During September and October, according to the Chinese lunar calendar, that is, the current October and November, female and male crabs mature respectively. The time that it takes for both female and male crabs to mature simultaneously is even shorter, no longer than 10 days, to be exact. So the best time for enjoying crabs is fleeting. When the season for crabs arrives, the *Dazha* crabs from Yangcheng Lake are flown to various cities so that people's appetites can be satisfied.

The Chinese people's love of crabs is time-honored— people eat crabs not only to fulfill their desire for food, they also see the spirit of eating crabs as a leisurely and carefree mood to which they aspire. "Enjoying

Dazha crabs from Yangcheng Lake are the best crabs in the mind of the Chinese people. Dazha crabs are usually tied up preferably with cotton thread before they are delivered to the market or cooked.

Fragrant and hot flavored crabs.

crabs," "drinking wine," "feasting their eyes on chrysanthemums" and "composing poems impromptu" are pleasant, indispensable golden autumn activities for ancient, learned Chinese men.

Cooking the delicious *Dazha* crabs is unusually easy—the crabs with purple perilla are put into boiling water over a roaring fire. Within 20 minutes at most, the once arrogant and ferocious crabs become the people's dish on the dinner table, their shells turning golden red and the meat brimming with fragrance. Crabs are associated with art and culture connoisseurs, yet it is difficult to maintain refined manners when eating them because retrieving all the shiny eggs and white meat from its shell is a huge, meticulous project. Today, most people resort to using both hands and teeth to conquer the likes of the *Dazha* crabs. This way of eating crabs is aggressive and unrestrained, but it will unavoidably cause some loss of the meat. As a matter of fact, the ancients had already invented professional tools for eating crabs, namely the "eight tools for eating crabs." It is said that the professionals who are skilled at using the "eight tools for eating crabs" can take all the meat out of the crab without damaging a single bite, and the crab can be restored to its original shape if the empty shells are pieced together.

As far as food goes, crabs are cold. In addition, people need to have vinegar mixed with minced ginger. Minced ginger and vinegar are capable of both adding flavor and dispelling the cold. People who are particular about how they eat crabs also need to have high-grade Shaoxing rice wine and, after they've had their fill, they finally have a cup of hot ginger tea, which warms their stomachs as well as their hearts.

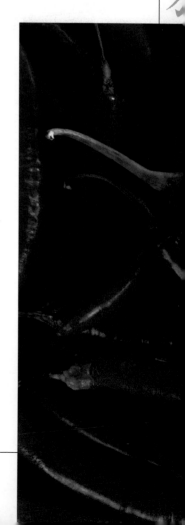

Sichuan Food—The Strongest Flavors in China

The "Eight Styles of Chinese Cuisine" include Shandong food, Sichuan food, Guangdong food, Fujian food, Jiangsu food, Zhejiang food, Hunan food and Anhui food. Each of the eight styles has its own merit and all are equally matched in taste and flavor. But when considering the widespread influence and popularity of these eight styles of Chinese cuisine among the Chinese people, Sichuan food will top the list.

The principal condiments served in Sichuan food consist of three items: chili, hot pepper and Chinese prickly ash. What is remarkable about Sichuan food is not limited to the singular numb-and-hot taste. As the saying goes, "Various combinations of five basic tastes

Flame-like red peppers.

will produce a hundred flavors." In other words, the five tastes of salty, sweet, numbing, hot and sour can produce a profuse variety of flavors like numb-and-hot taste, bitter fragrant, home cooking, salty and refreshing, fish, lychee and even other interesting flavors. According to statistics, there are 23 traditional flavors in Sichuan food. The flavors of the new-style Sichuan food, which has been developed in the past few years by adopting qualities from other regions, number over 40. Aside from its "wide-ranging flavors," Sichuan food attaches greater importance to "strong taste." Sichuan people have almost reached the limit in pursuing and worshipping flavors, as if nothing except strong flavors can do justice to their sense of taste. Compared with Guangdong-style food, which advocates retaining food's original flavor, the guiding principle of Sichuan food is that the food will do battle with you until you can no longer taste the original flavors of the raw, unrefined ingredients. Whichever flavor it may be, it does not allow your tongue access to any other flavor. You can do nothing but resign yourself to the overwhelmingly rich, strong essence.

Talented Sichuan chefs who specialize in Sichuan-style food are growing in large numbers; 1,000 Sichuan people can come up with 1,000 classic Sichuan dishes. Nevertheless, among all these classics, a few deserve special attention. "Twice-cooked pork" and "*Mapo* bean curd" are two such instances. There is nothing unusual in the appearance of twice-cooked pork. The pork is first cooked and then fried. As simple and unadorned as this method seems, it demands an extremely precise duration and degree of cooking. When Sichuan people who have been living outside Sichuan for a long time return home, the dish that first comes to their minds is the twice-cooked pork. The name of "*Mapo* bean curd" stems from the marks on the face of Grandma Chen, the inventor of the dish. Amidst the minced chili and fresh gravy, the tender, delicate bean curd and the crisp, minced beef give off an appetizing aroma. Camphorwood and tea-smoked duck, totally absent the smell of smoke and fire, gives off

Red peppers getting
dried in a peasant's
courtyard.

a profound delicate flavor. It was once used by Premier
Zhou Enlai to entertain Sir Charles Chaplin. Stir-fried,
diced chicken with chili and peanuts originated from
an official's family of the Qing Dynasty. Fish-flavored
shredded pork is a "grassroots dish of great renown"
known to every household. All the aforementioned
dishes are shining examples of the Sichuan-style dishes
prepared through the "various combinations of the
five basic tastes." The last item worthy of attention is
a rising star—water-boiled fish. Only in the past five
years has this dish come to the forefront, but it has swept
the country with amazing speed. The fiery chili and
white fish slices, spreading as quickly as an epidemic,
conquered everyone from all corners of China, the first
being Beijing, and challenged people to re-think the size
of their food containers, their resistance to the amount
of oil used, their imagination about the extensiveness of
chili and their ultimate tolerance for the numb-and-hot

taste.

The mystery and wonder of Sichuan style food rest on its vigorous vitality and powerful appeal to people. From the "Chengdu Snacks," which are ubiquitous, to fancy restaurants with names like "South the Beautiful," of which reputation seems more significant than the food itself, Sichuan food can be not only simple, but also complex, not only tradition-oriented but also fashion-oriented. In Beijing, Sichuan-style restaurants are always overcrowded; customers are forever standing and waiting for seats in restaurants with a "name." Considering the eager anticipation and high expectations on their faces, it cannot be denied that Sichuan food has the strongest flavors in China.

Classical Sichuan-style dishes—twice-cooked pork and stir-fried diced chicken with chili and peanuts.

Crossing the Bridge—Rice-flour Noodles in the Manner of Yunnan

Yunnan, literally meaning "South of the Colorful Clouds," is like spring year-round; flowers bloom in all seasons. Among the sketches of Yunnan local customs and sceneries entitled "Eighteen Wonders in Yunnan," the 17th wonder falls on "Crossing the Bridge—Rice-flour Noodles in the Manner of Yunnan is loved by all." This saying is in no way an overstatement. Once you've had a bowl of rice-flour noodles, you'll know instantly how delicious it is.

Like almost all the local snacks in China, rice-flour noodles in the manner of Yunnan are associated with a moving tale. Popular legend has it that in the suburbs of the town Mengzi, Yunnan was a lake called Nanhu. In

Crossing the bridge rice-flour noodles are made of rice-flour noodles and chicken soup, along with various assortments. This food with a strong Yunnan flavor has swept the country.

the center of Nanhu Lake was a small island on which thick forests and tall bamboo grew. This small island was a nice place to read and study. During the Qing Dynasty, a *xiucai* (a person who passed the imperial examination at the county level during the Ming and Qing dynasties) whose surname was Yang read and studied poems and ancient classics every day on this island. His wife would take his favorite food, rice-flour noodles, to him every day by way of a stone bridge that led to the island. As it was a long way, the rice-flour noodles often were cold by the time they reached him. One day, Yang's wife cooked a pot of chicken soup for him and, to her surprise, she found that the chicken soup was as hot as ever. Upon closer examination, she realized that a film of oil on the soup had kept it warm. Enlightened by this, the wife made this kind of chicken soup often from then on. She brought with her the cooked rice-flour noodles, sliced pork and vegetables, and, when she reached the stone bridge, she put all these into the chicken soup to heat them. When this bowl of noodles reached Yang, it was just ready to be served. Yang finally succeeded in passing the imperial examinations at higher levels and became an official. However, what is more praiseworthy than his scholarly honor and official rank is this bowl of rice-flour noodles.

The ready-made rice-flour noodles *a la* Yunnan, beautifully colored, taste delicious. One can never get tired of eating them.

Nowadays, more attention is given to the soup, the raw and unrefined materials and the ways of eating the noodles. The soup can be made of either chicken, duck or pork bones. It is clear and has a pleasantly strong taste, yet it does not overshadow the original flavors of the other food contained in the bowl of rice-flour noodles. The meat for rice-flour noodles comprises chicken breast, snake-headed fish, squid, pig tenderloin, pig liver, pig kidney, ham, etc., all of which are made into slices as thin as cicada's wings. Vegetables for rice-flour noodles include spinach, pea sprouts, yellow Chinese chives, soybean milk and hydrated bamboo shoots, all which are fresh and tender. Ground pepper and boiled chicken oil are poured into a deep bowl, then boiling soup is poured in; a film of oil will surface and envelop the soup. The soup appears calm, but is like a scorching fire within. The meat, vegetables and rice-flour noodles are placed into the soup and thus heated before it is served. Those who are fussy about eating this food also follow "crossing the bridge" when adding the rice-flour noodles: they move the bowl of noodles closer to the soup bowl, make a bridge of the noodles between the bowls, and then move the noodles into the soup bowl without interruption. Compared with the process of "crossing the bridge," the practice of just pouring the noodles whole into the soup is not worthy of the charm of the expression "crossing the bridge."

Mutton with Baked Buns—The True Spirit Exclusive to the Loess Plateau

Xi'an used to be an ancient capital of China, bearing association with an outlook of being simple, unadorned, unconstrained and bold. The terracotta warriors of the Qin Dynasty are historical records of Xianyang of 2,000 years ago, while Huaqing Pool in present-day Xi'an (a spa favored by the Tang Imperial Concubine Yang Guifei) relates the stories about Chang'an, the capital of the Tang Dynasty 1,000 years ago. But, to get acquainted with the real Xi'an today and to thoroughly understand the people presently living there, different aspects of Xi'an life and the true spirit exclusive to Xi'an focus on a bowl of mutton with baked

A view of the Loess Plateau in northern Shaanxi.

Mutton with Baked Buns, containing plenty of foodstuff and strong soup, are highly nourishing.

buns.

When arriving at a restaurant that specializes in mutton with baked buns, take a large white porcelain bowl, which is acclaimed as "Number One Bowl under Heaven"—the rim is as large as a human head— and get two baked buns. Stroll first around the other customers who are breaking up the buns easily and those who are drinking their hot soup. By the time you get a seat, your appetite and eagerness will have been fully whetted by the customers who are all smiles and dripping with sweat.

When having mutton with baked buns, break up the buns yourself. The buns, which are 90 percent dough and 10 percent unleavened dough, are first formed into buns and then baked—crisp, crunchy, sweet and delicious. The buns need to be broken into pieces that are as small as the heads of bees. Only by doing so can the buns become

51

tasty, chewy and smooth.

The small pieces are then taken to the kitchen. The cook responsible for the assortment deftly slices prepared, streaky mutton, readies some vermicelli made of bean starch, dried bean curd, edible black fungus, garlic shoot, etc., spreads chopped green onion and coriander on it and then passes it on to the master chef, who's been waiting by the stove. The master chef takes a spoonful of leftover sauce from a pot to the frying pan. When the sauce begins to boil, the chef empties everything into the pan and boils the mixture thoroughly over a roaring fire; this way, mutton with baked buns can be served instantly. The leftover sauce is made of mutton, sheep bones and various condiments. The mutton is thoroughly cooked while the sauce is thick and sticky. The well-cooked mutton is taken from the pot and reserved for later use,

Guokui (Hard Wheat Cake) is a kind of large cake peculiar to northwest China.

while the sauce is used for making mutton with baked buns. In the frying pan where the mutton with baked buns is cooked, the leftover sauce and the prepared, streaky mutton meet again. As a result, all the different flavors are stored in the buns, making them chewy, sticky and strongly aromatic.

People usually have mutton with baked buns to accompany pepper, coriander and sweetened garlic, nibbled from the rim of the bowl. Thus, the flavor of the leftover sauce is well-preserved to produce a lingering scent. In no time, customers will feel hot and beads of sweat will cover their foreheads. Another bowl of the original leftover sauce after a bowl of mutton with baked buns will satisfy and energize the customers.

When Xi'an people drink their soup, they are eager and anxious, but when they are breaking up the buns, they assume a languor—a free and leisurely attitude. This striking contrast between impatient anxiety and languorous ease illustrates the distinct way of life of the people living on the loess plateau.

Northeast Style Dishes Are like Old Friends

People from the northeast are rustic and rough. Men are usually bold and unrestrained by nature while women can be fractious. In the depths of winter, the breath can turn into ice. Despite this, the winter is still the best season to go sightseeing in the northeast and to enjoy the food. When going to a peasant's house in the northeast, carry a bottle of top-quality liquor and tread all the way on top of the snow, because the host will surely invite you into his *kang* clay bed to warm your feet. Sitting around a brazier and chitchatting, you'll find lots of fragrant northeast style food being placed on the *kang* table.

Of all northeast dishes, northeast sheet jelly is often the first course served. Sheet jelly is made from bean or sweet potato starch, sparkling and clear, smooth and chewy. Sheet jelly is cut into broad slices, added with shredded cucumbers, shredded carrots, shredded pork, and coriander and mashed garlic. Then this colorful dish is ready to be served.

The basic dish in northeast style food is prepared by

A world of ice and snow.

The warm *kang* clay bed in a peasant's home in northeast China.

stewing. People from the northeast love stewed food, mixed stew (or medley) in particular. Mixed stew is made by putting whatever food, vegetables and meat one likes into a pot at once and stews them. The representative dish of northeast style food is stewed pork, which is very popular among peasant families. At the end of the year, each family kills a pig and makes sausage with pig blood. The pork is then cut into large cubes and stewed in a pot together with bones, offal, pickled vegetables, vermicelli made from bean starch, frozen bean curd, etc. When it is finished, all the neighbors will be invited to share the dish, presenting a splendid scene. The famous northeast dish at present is "Stewed Pork with Vermicelli," the exquisite and improved popular version of the stewed pork. The well-cooked, streaky pork is sliced; the vermicelli is steeped and softened in water, and the pickled vegetables are cut into shreds and stewed in pork bone soup. The longer they are stewed, the more delicious they taste.

Stewed chicken with mushrooms is another famous dish of the northeast stewed food. As a common practice, a mother-in-law from the northeast uses this dish to treat her new son-in-law. So, naturally this dish is often made more exquisitely and carefully than the stewed pork with vermicelli, which is usually done for the father-in-law as a dish to accompany wine. The chicken used for this dish is domestic and eats all kinds of food grains; the mushrooms are hazel mushrooms collected from the Changbai Mountains, with small, umbrella-shaped tops and long handles, giving off a delicate fragrance of the wilderness. The new son-in-law will already be transported by the flavor of the stewed chicken with mushrooms before it is even served.

After eating stewed food, people feel warm inside and out. Then they can take a thick bone seasoned with soy sauce with both hands and enjoy the marrow. What follows is a dish named "three seasonal vegetable delicacies," which is made of potatoes, peppers and eggplant. Potatoes taste soft; peppers, crisp; and the eggplant, sweet in the aftertaste.

Having enjoyed the northeast dishes, people also need to have a taste of peasants' home cooking. The northeast abounds with corn and there are over a dozen refreshments made from corn flour. A bowl of fragrant, sweet corn porridge and corn buns will be served as the last course to complete a perfect meal.

When having meals at peasants' homes, apart from feeling free to have your fill, don't make excuses when it comes to drinking wine or liquor, as people from the northeast are heavy drinkers. For them, "bottoms up" is a high priority. The warm-hearted, uninhibited people from the northeast, in many ways similar to their well-cooked northeast food, are sincere and honest, though not dazzling and ostentatious. Take them as your friends upon the first meeting and take them also as lifelong friends.

Soup—Source to a Happier Life

People throughout the world share almost the same view on drinking soup. The French love to drink onion soup, the Americans love to drink chicken soup, the Germans love to drink beer soup, the English people love to drink curry soup, and the Russians love to drink borscht. The Chinese are also fond of drinking soup. In China, a bowl of soup serves not only as a "cupful of a snack" before a meal, but is also a symbol of "home" and bridges affection among family members. A bowl of long-cooked soup on the dinner table will kindle the feeling of having returned home. A bowl of sweet soup served after returning home at midnight will dispel all the day's frustrations. Soup is the timely rain that saturates the lives of the Chinese people.

Many kinds of soup can be found in China: clear soup, meat soup, thick-and-strong soup, broth and sweet soup. Cooking clear soup does not take long; meat soup takes a little longer; and thick and strong soup takes the longest. When making broth, starch is often used to thicken it,

Folk earthen jar soup is stewed in an especially-made large jar according to the traditional recipe over a slow fire.

Chicken soup is of great nutritional value.

and, for sweet soup, no meat is used. Of all these, meat soup can be eaten as a main dish, sweet soup is often used as a midnight snack, clear soup, thick-and-strong soup and broths are good companions of various food and dishes. The most frequently seen soup on dinner tables includes chicken soup, fish soup and bone soup. Chicken soup can serve to keep away a chill, fish soup can prove effective in curing asthma and bone soup can compensate for a calcium deficiency, demonstrating the healthful benefits of drinking soup, which the Chinese people believe implicitly. Soup can be made of meat, vegetables, beans, fruits and even all kinds of grasses. The utensil that is best suited for cooking soup is a sand pot made of pottery clay and fine sand. Of all the food utensils, the sand pot heats the slowest and is the most balanced in gathering heat, and the best in retaining heat and keeping the temperature constant for the longest time. The heat it carries is moderate and lasting. Soup cooked in a sand pot is not just intoxicatingly delicious, but its nutritional value is preserved to the fullest. Generally, almost all soup is stewed over a slow fire. The Chinese are not in favor of extremes or acting uncontrollably. The way of making soup in China—over a neither too strong nor too weak a fire, neither too quickly nor too slowly—represents the very essence of the Chinese people, who advocate being moderate and pursuing the golden mean.

Generally, soup can be divided into northern soup and southern soup, the former stressing color, fragrance and taste; the latter stressing concept, form and nutrition.

In Henan Province, people greet each other by saying, "Have you drunk soup?" instead of "Have you had your meal?" In Luoyang, two out of the three meals of each day are addressed as "drinking soup." Among the elderly Luoyang people is the saying, "Bean curd soup in the morning and meatball soup in the evening." Luoyang Soup Banquet, Luoyang Peony and Longmen Grottoes compose the "Three Wonders of Luoyang." Luoyang Soup has a history of over 1,000 years and Luoyang people always entertain their guests with soup banquets on major occasions, such as weddings and funerals. It is called "soup banquet" for two reasons: one is that the procession in which the dishes are successively brought to the table can be likened to floating clouds and running streams, and the other is that each of the dishes contain soup and juice within. The last course of a soup banquet is egg soup, which is jokingly called by the local people "get out soup," for the arrival of egg soup means that all the dishes have been served and the banquet will soon be over. This is also common practice in many other regions, where soup is regarded as the grand finale of a dinner. Soup is like a ceremony without speeches, as well as cheerful.

Nourishing stewed food is widely favored by all.

Southern soup is headed by Guangdong soup. Guangdong people, just like Shanxi people who have no vinegar or Sichuan people who have no peppers for a whole day, will feel uncomfortable if they don't have soup all day. Guangdong people love soup and are good at making it as well. The ingredients they use are usually purchased from Chinese medicine stores. These include items such as *fructus amomis*, which helps to regulate the stomach, Chinese *angelica* which enriches the blood and regulates the *qi, fuling,* which soothes the nerves, apricot nuts, which reduces phlegm and stops coughing, the blossom of crab cactus, which relieves fever and moistens the lungs, sea-bottom copra, which softens the skin and enhances beauty, and so on. Most Guangdong soup is thick and strong and the principal ingredient is usually meat. Also, different soups differ in terms of function: mutton is warm, chicken moderate and duck cold. The arrangement of the principal food and other assortments should be done according to the principle of regulating the *yin* and the *yang*, depending on the season. Moreover, the arrangement also needs adjustment according to people's physiques. Those who have excessive internal heat are not compatible with ginseng, while those who suffer from internal cold are not compatible with green beans. Most people from the north take it for granted that soup will be fresh and delicious without condiments. This concept leads to their massive use of onions, ginger, Chinese prickly ash, aniseed, gourmet powder and cooking wine. Actually, for Guangdong people, a single piece of ginger is sufficient to make a pot of soup, as what they seek is nothing but the original taste. In Guangdong, soup signals not the end of the meal, but the beginning. Guangdong people are used to having soup before the meal; otherwise, they find it difficult to gobble down the food. In Guangdong and Hong Kong, what men and women cherish most is the strong aroma emanating from a pot of slowly cooked soup. For this reason, each girl firmly believes that she will not have a happy family unless she fully knows the art of making soup.

An Array of Dishes of the Manchu and Han Can Take Three Days to Eat

Perhaps no place in the world has as many first-rate meals as China. The highest achievement of the idea that "food is the first necessity of man" can be found in an array of dishes of the Manchu and Han—the finest expression of Chinese cuisine.

Dishes of the Manchu and Han nationalities, as the name suggests, is the combination of the classic dishes from the Manchu and Han nationalities. Stemming from the period of the Qing Dynasty (1616–1911), it originally referred to an official feast shared by both the Manchu people and Han people. The term "an array of dishes of the Manchu and Han" sounds as though it was the outcome of the arrival of northern nomadic tribes in the central plains, but actually it originated from the meals

The array of dishes of the Manchu and Han shows the extensiveness and profundily of Chinese food culture.

popular in the official circles in south China. It is said that the dishes of the Manchu and Han was, in the beginning, offered by the local officials of Yangzhou to entertain the senior officials from the imperial palace. Taking advantage of the beautiful scenery of Yangzhou from where many outstanding people came, including experienced and knowledgeable Yangzhou chefs, the dishes of the Manchu and Han witnessed rapid, wide development. Emperor Qianlong altogether visited south China six times. Yangzhou officials and gentry greeted Emperor Qianlong with the array of dishes of the Manchu and Han six times. Since then, the dishes have become known far and wide and was imitated everywhere. By and by, the region formed the established dishes and a protocol of its own.

The dishes were first used to treat the senior officials after the imperial examination ended. Just imagine the scene when the highest local official entertained the imperial commissioners. At the feast, all officials, regardless of their ranks, were in their ceremonial robes and official hats. The dishes were abundant and exquisite, the protocol solemn and complicated. How grand and sumptuous the feast must have been! There are strict rules and regulations in respect of the spectacle and scale of the feast, of the official ranks and number of people who accompany them at the table, and of the variety and quantity of the dishes. The ceremonies such as the firing of guns, playing music, burning joss-sticks, welcoming and seeing off senior officials and the like are as meticulous as can be. There are at least 108 dishes, soup, refreshments and fruit on the table, and it usually takes people three days to eat such an array of dishes.

It is by no means an overstatement to say that the dishes represent an encyclopedia of Chinese food. Included in these dishes are imperial delicacies and local snacks, marked by features of two different nationalities and characteristics of the seasons. The array of dishes is all-embracing: cold dishes, cooked dishes, meat dishes and vegetable dishes. Some taste sour, some hot, some

Dining hall with an air of antiquity

salty and some sweet; some are fried in shallow oil, some stir-fried, some quick-fried and some deep-fried. The dishes include birds, beasts, mountain delicacies and sea-food delights. Though it might sound daunting to "read" this encyclopedia in just three days, the taste buds would surely shout "bravo!" if it could speak.

In order to restore the original elements of these dishes, the Imperial Dishes Restaurant of Beijing made extensive inquiries and conducted textual research all over China and re-wrote the menu, which included 196 cold and cooked dishes, 124 refreshments and cookies. The array of dishes of the Manchu and Han was subdivided into "Banquet in Vassal States' Honor," "Banquet in Honor of Courtiers," "Longevity Banquet," "Banquet in Honor of His Highness," "Nine-White Banquet" and "Seasonal Banquet." As this array of dishes had done in the past, preparing them according to the original menu took people three days and six separate sessions to finish eating it. Pu Jie, the brother of the last emperor Pu Yi, described this in his own writing, "Authentic Food for the Emperor" after he had tasted the dishes. If you have the ambition and strength to acquire the heavy reinforcement of Chinese food and if you believe you have a large enough appetite, try it!

The Fragrance and Delightful Taste of Tea

Small Teahouses Hold All Things Possible under the Sun

*T*he *Teahouse* written by Lao She is a classic work in the history of Chinese drama. The small Yutai Teahouse portrayed in this work is just a stage on which the changes of time unfold, giving us a vivid picture of the people from all walks of life. The success of *The Teahouse* rests not only with the story, but also with the special medium of the story, the teahouse, because a teahouse is indeed a place of wonder.

From time immemorial, teahouses have been regarded as the common space in the lives of people. The doors of

Laoshe Teahouse in front of Qianmen in Beijing.

Teahouses are miniatures of Chinese tea culture and the major places where the Chinese people spend their leisure times.

teahouses are open to all people, whether they are travellers arriving and leaving hastily or guests strolling in leisurely, regardless of their social status. There is definitely more to drinking tea when people visit a teahouse. The possible purposes of their visits to the teahouses might be to pose as lovers of art and culture, mingle with the literati, entertain themselves, make friends, debate, conduct deals or meet a hero of rivers and lakes. Patrons of teahouses include officials, peasants, workers, businessmen, Confucian scholars, monks, Taoists and Buddhists. A teahouse is where both the most philistine and the most refined are accommodated, where people can be the busiest at work and at the same time at their most easygoing and carefree. Their forefathers once said, "Hermits reside among the mountains and woods, while sages reside in the downtown areas." Visiting teahouses in downtown areas is the way of life of the "sages."

"Pure teahouses" in old Beijing principally offered

tea. Ranging from the elderly citizens who took walks in the early morning to the peddlers who had just finished work. People came and went in an endless stream: some holding different kinds of birdcages, some with news from different corners, some with their knack of drinking tea as well as doing business, and also some carrying troubles of their own families. Besides "pure teahouses" in Beijing there are also "storytelling teahouses," "opera fun teahouses," "chess players teahouses," etc. "Rural teahouse," a thatched cottage offering ordinary tea in large bowls, is the outcome of the imperial families' outings. Strongly imbued with an idyllic appeal, it gives tea drinkers the feeling of having returned to nature. Today, "Lao She Teahouse" in Beijing has developed into a grand teahouse that embraces the tea ceremony, tea banquet, opera, folk art, magic, acrobatics, fine imperial refreshments and local snacks.

Chengdu, Sichuan is regarded as the place of origin of "the life of idlers." When Huang Yanpei (a democratic patriot of modern China) was visiting Chengdu, he wrote two lines of comic verse, "When one is idle, he counts the flagstones of the pavement. When two are free, they

Aged frequent visitors of old teahouses, chatting freely over a cup of tea.

Teahouses, beautifully decorated and possessing cultural ethos, are the major places for entertainments in modern cities.

stay in a teahouse from morning till night." For Chengdu people, there is nothing odd about staying in a teahouse from morning till night. Chengdu people call chitchatting "spinning a yarn." The subject-matter of "spinning a yarn" in a teahouse are all-encompassing, ranging from astronomy to geography, from state policies to household affairs, from the past to the present, in short, everything under the sun. Here, learned men can recite poetry and paint and amateur performers of local operas can entertain themselves by singing and observing others. One can find a barber and have a haircut, find a pedicurist to do his feet, buy food from the peddlers and ask a fortune-teller to reveal his future. The water on the stove boils day and night. Moreover, a tea drinker can even come here and wash his face in the morning after getting out of bed and wash his feet before going to bed. If he has something urgent to attend to, he'll rise, push his tea bowl into the center of the table and tell the waiter, "I'll be back soon." Upon his return, he'll continue to drink the same bowl of tea.

Tea art performance.

In addition, tea drinkers can enjoy the Chinese zither in Yangzhou teahouses, storytelling combined with ballad singing in Suzhou teahouses, both tea and the beautiful scenery in Hangzhou and tea along with all sorts of refreshments in Guangzhou... As Chinese tea culture is extensive and profound, teahouse cultures in different places of China vary greatly, too.

Quality Tea Has Always Been like a Beautiful Woman

Seven things of principal importance to the Chinese people are "firewood, rice, oil, salt, soy sauce, vinegar and tea." The first six are more or less related to food. There is nothing strange about it, as "food is the first necessity of man." The most important thing is tea. This clearly reveals how important tea is in the lives of the Chinese people. Drinking tea is not solely to quench the thirst, to become refreshed, to energize the mind and to help the digestive process; it is also a way of life that has been firmly established. In China there are 16 provinces, including Taiwan Province, that produce tea. In the light of different tea-processing methods, tea is classified into six major types, namely, green tea, black tea, oolong tea, white tea (a kind of unfermented or unbaked and unrolled tea, made by a special process), yellow tea and dark tea. In each type of tea is a top quality tea handed down from ancient times, for instance, *longjing* (Dragon

Places that enjoy special favors of nature in natural environment can often produce best quality tea which is hard to come by

Well) in the type of green tea, *keemun* in black tea, *tieguan-yin* in oolong tea, white-haired silver needles in white tea, Junshan silver needles in yellow tea and *pu'er* in dark tea. Of all these types, green tea has the longest history, the greatest output and the greatest number of drinkers. In addition, green tea is the one best-loved among tea drinkers.

The West Lake of Hangzhou is the homeland of *longjing* tea. Places by West Lake, such as Shifeng, Longjing, Yunqi, Hupao, Tianzhu and Lingyin, are located among the ranges of mountains with tall, ancient trees and green bamboo, which are veiled in clouds and mists. The climate is humid and warm year-round. The *longjing* tea trees grow in the beautiful landscape of lake and mountains and are luxuriantly green throughout the whole year. Young buds of tea leaves on the *longjing* tea trees blossom uninterruptedly from spring to autumn, and the leaves can be picked as often as 30 times a year. The tea picked before "pure brightness" (April 5 or 6) called "prior to brightness tea," is the best. The tea picked before the "grain rain" (April 20 or 21), called "prior to rain tea," is second best. It usually needs thousands of fine and tender buds of tea leaves to process one *jin* of best quality "prior to brightness tea." A saying in the hometowns of tea goes, "Women pick tea and men process tea." The art of processing tea rests in a pair of hands. There are as many as over a dozen ways to process tea. To make *longjing* tea, which is the best qualified in color, fragrance, taste and shape, demands not only superb skill but also full concentration of the person who processes it. All the top quality *longjing* tea is prepared by hand. *Longjing* tea is clear, bright and has a refreshing, lingering fragrance.

Biluochun tea, world famous for its beautiful shape, brilliant color, strong fragrance and pure taste, is the product of the Dongting Mountains by the Taihu Lake of Wuxian County, Jiangsu Province. The two hills of the Dongting Mountains, one stretching to the east, the other to the west, are beautiful with green woods and clear

Left: Fine and thick hairs on the new tender shoots of *longjing* tea.

Right: Stir-frying tea needs manual skill.

water and are humid year-round. Here, tea trees and fruit trees such as peach trees, plum trees, apricot trees and Chinese plum trees are hybridized. The fragrance of the different fruit seeps into the tea leaves, which results in the tea's natural pleasant smell. The time for picking *biluochun* starts around vernal equinox (March 21 or 20) and lasts till grain rain. Usually, the first shoots and first leaves are picked for *biluochun*. A historical record has it that one *jin* of *biluochun* consisted of 90,000 young tea shoots, which revealed how tender the tea leaves were. The skill of frying tea rests with the hands that never leave the tea; the tea never leaves the frying pan. Rubbing the tea and frying the tea is done simultaneously. The fried *biluochun* appears thin, twisted and hairy. First, boiled water is poured into the cup before the tea is added. The tea sinks to the bottom of the cup quickly and the white thin hair of the tea begins to unfurl in the water. Instantly, the bottom of the cup turns green, emitting a pleasant fragrance. The word *bi* (碧) , meaning bright green, indicates its color; the word *luo* (螺), meaning spiral shell, indicates its shape; and the word *chun* (春), meaning spring, refers to its fragrance and the image it

Longjing (Dragon Well) to the west of the West Lake.
Longjing tea got its name from Longjing.

A tea worker plucking new tea leaves.

inspires in the drinkers, such as the early spring in south China—pleasant spring scenery and intoxicating spring breeze.

The places of origin of Huangshan *Maofeng* and Lushan *Yunwu* are both mountains of great renown. The Huangshan Mountain is world famous for its "pine trees and hills of immense shapes and appearances, mists of a sea of clouds and hot springs." Lushan Mountain has the good reputation that "In spring the Lushan Mountain is dreamlike, in summer emerald green, in autumn intoxicating and enthralling and in winter like white jade." These two mountains are veiled in mists and clouds throughout the year and the tea trees there are thoroughly saturated with moistness, free from cold and heat and draw miraculous powers from heaven and earth. Huangshan *Maofeng* tea takes the shape of sparrow tongues and emits a lovely gardenia scent. Lushan *Yunwu* tea is beautiful, possessing a sweet aroma and pungent fragrance. When it is prepared for drinking, Lushan *Yunwu* tea, setting forth a pungent, lingering fragrance, also appears as misty as the Lushan Mountain.

Famous mountains do not necessarily produce quality tea, but all kinds of quality tea usually grow in famous mountains. Two more kinds of quality tea, Lu'an *Guapian* (Lu'an Melon Seeds) and Xinyang *Maojian* (Xingyang Young Tender Shoots), also come from the Dabie Mountain, which stretches 270 km long and is unbroken. Lu'an *Guapian* tea, made of only tender leaves, exclusive of buds and stems, is smooth, flat and resembles melon seeds in shape; hence, its name. The frying process of Lu'an *Guapian* tea undergoes two stages. First, it is fried in a high-temperature pot and fried for the second time in a lower-temperature pot. These two pots stand side by side, tilted,

The newly-plucked tea leaves from the Wuyi Mountains.

facing each other, which presents an interesting tableau. Different from the tea-frying method practised in Suzhou and Hangzhou, which mainly relies on a pair of hands, tea-frying in the Dabie Mountain area is usually done by using bamboo blooms and reed-spike blooms. The movements of the frying process—turning, rubbing, throwing and shaking the leaves—are as graceful as long-sleeve dancing. Xinyang *Maojian* tea is folded, tight and sharp. It appears yellowish when made with boiled water and tastes refreshing. The time for picking Xinyang *Maojian* usually begins between mid-April and the last 10 days of April. It is said that in ancient times top-quality Xinyang *Maojian* was picked only by girls 15 or 16 years old, and before picking, these girls had to bathe and change their clothes. Then they had to pick the young tea shoots with their mouths and place them into the perfumed pouches hanging in front of their chests. When enjoying this tea, the purity and refined spirits of the Xinyang girls can be felt.

The famous line from one of Su Dongpo's poems has long been known: "I would rather compare the West Lake to the Beauty Xishi." But most people are not aware that he also had another line that draws an analogy to a beauty: "Quality tea has always been like a beautiful woman." Like a beautiful woman, the refined and graceful sentiments in top-quality tea also spring from nature.

The Sweet Fragrance of Spring Wafting from Tea

Though tea is just an everyday beverage, it has a unique personality of its own. People from the north are fond of jasmine tea, which tastes fragrant and strong. People from the south prefer green tea. People from the provinces in southwest China are used to drinking *pu'er* tea, which has a pure and unadulterated taste. People from Fujian, Guangdong and Taiwan Provinces love to make "kung fu tea" with oolong tea. Herdsmen from the pastures need to drink milk tea, which is made by boiling horse milk, cow milk, and ewe milk together with fermented brick tea. People say that green tea represents the character of the literati in south China—slightly bitter, simple but profound; black tea has the character of a young lady—quiet and leisurely; oolong tea symbolizes the senior people's wisdom—unsophisticated, mellow and full; while jasmine tea seems like

Bright-colored tea.

the philistines—buzzing with activity, thick, strong and straightforward. In light of this, judging by what kind of tea a person drinks, a rough idea can be gleaned about where he lives, as well as his individual personality and sense of taste.

Tea drinking in different regions is not only marked by distinct, local characteristics, but also by the different times that tea is drunk during the day. If it is assumed that green tea is a good for giving a boost at 10 o'clock in the morning, drinking black tea is then the most adequate choice after 3 o'clock in the afternoon. In the warmth and fragrance of a cup of afternoon black tea, the body and mind is slowly relieved of lethargy.

As black tea is fermented, the black tea that is made in boiled water is of different shades of red: warm in quality, thick and strong in taste, and pure and sweet in smell.

Tea workers sifting and selecting black tea leaves.

Black tea in bags has won the favor of office workers for its convenience.

The earliest black tea in China, which was grown in the place of happiness for tea, the Wuyi Mountains, came into existence in Fujian Province in the 16th century. In the beginning, this type of tea was known as "small seed black tea," and the "Zhengshan small seed" produced in the northern part of the Wuyi Mountains was regarded as authentic. Small seed black tea should possess the aroma of the smoked pinewood and appear like the longan soup when made in boiled water. In the mid-18th century, small seed black tea evolved into "kung fu black tea," which instantly became popular in many parts of China and was sold overseas. The processing technique of kung fu black tea was then passed to India, Sri Lanka and other countries, where "crushed black tea" was derived. The leaves of crushed black tea are in bits and scraps, tasting fresh and strong when made in boiled water. Sugar and milk are often added to the crushed black tea, and, by doing so, the crushed black tea is made more suited to the taste and usual practice of the Western people. In addition to this, it is also appropriate for tea in bags.

Many people's knowledge about black tea is limited to Lipton's Yellow Label Tea, and they don't know that the highly honored British tea culture had been set out to sea from Fujian, China and then passed to the British Isles. While the English gentlemen were adding sugar and milk to their silver teacups on a misty afternoon, the Chinese were still holding fast to the traditions that had lasted for 1,000 years, enjoying kung fu tea with ease and leisure with mini-sized Yixing teapots. The two words "kung fu" in kung fu tea refer to both the kung fu (the skill) required in tea processing and the kung fu (the period of time) spent on tea drinking. The process of tea processing covers withering, rubbing, fermenting and drying, which naturally takes time. Tea drinking should also follow the practice of being fully and slowly sipped. First, its shade should be appreciated; second, its pleasant fragrance should be enjoyed; and, finally, its taste should be savored. There are various homes to kung fu black tea: Fujian is home to *Min* kung fu black tea, Sichuan home to *Chuan* kung fu black tea, Jiangxi home to *Ning* kung fu black tea and Guangdong is home to *Yue* kung fu black tea. However, *Dian hong* (*Dian* black tea) produced in Yunnan and *Qi hong* (*Qi* black tea) produced in Anhui are the two that have long enjoyed the greatest reputation. *Dian hong* tea is pleasantly strong, mellow and full. A gold ring always appears on the surface of the best quality *Dian hong*. *Qi hong* is among the top 10 famous brands of tea in China. Only when it is drunk slowly and quietly can its freshness, sweetness, fragrance and unusual charm be felt. Best-quality *Qi hong* often send off an aroma of orchids and roses. People from the west call this aroma *Qimen* fragrance. The English people like to drink *Qi hong* most, saying, "In the aroma of Chinese tea, we can feel the scent of spring."

The Marvel on Horseback

The world famous *pu'er* tea was actually the result of a wonderful mistake. The first flat cake of *pu'er* tea took shape on a jolting horseback ride amidst the long tickling of the horse bell. Tradition has it that during Emperor Qianlong's reign (1736–1796) of the Qing Dynasty, *Pu'er* prefecture of Yunnan paid tea tribute to the imperial court every year. One year, it was exceedingly wet. As the time to pay tribute was drawing close, the shipment of the tea started before it had been air-dried. It

Deep horse-hoof prints formed for years on end on an ancient tea-horse road.

was a two-to-three month journey from Yunnan to Beijing (the capital of the Qing Dynasty). The tea cakes carried on horseback had fermented during this time, but the bright, reddish tea made with it won the favor of Emperor Qianlong, who then bestowed it the name "*Pu'er* tea."

Aside from the round, flat, cake-shaped tea, *pu'er* tea is also made into various other shapes, such as bowl-shaped *tuo* tea, square-shaped brick tea, bar-shaped *qianliang* tea, half-melon-shaped, gold-melon and tribute tea. The main purpose of pressing the tea into various shapes is to transport more easily. The non-pressed tea is usually for local tea-drinkers. *Pu'er* tea can be classified according to the shapes it takes; also, it can be further classified into prepared tea and unprepared tea, according to different processing methods. Prepared tea is accomplished by adding water to and heating the tea to make it ferment rapidly through the reaction of moist and heat. Unprepared tea is cold in quality and harsh in flavor. It should be preserved for a long time in a dry storehouse, and aged and matured slowly and naturally over the course of years. The lifespan of top-quality *pu'er* tea can be dozens of years or even close to 100 years. Over the long years, *pu'er* tea gains the fresh aroma of camphor wood,

Quality *pu'er* tea cakes have distinct veins and are rich in fragrance.

the pleasantly sweet perfume of lotus and the sweet fragrance of orchids. Keeping a *pu'er*

tea cake for yourself for an extended period is a continuation of the life journey of the *pu'er* tea. As reading text is like a re-creation of the work being read, keeping *pu'er* tea itself is also like a re-creation of *pu'er* tea. This characteristic of *pu'er*'s worthy cache creates a miraculous affinity between *pu'er* tea and red wine. Similar to red wine, *pu'er* tea is closely associated with its origin and age, and the way that it is stored. It is red, resembling the color of red wine, and tastes sweet and refreshing. People even enjoy *pu'er* tea the same way as they enjoy red wine. *Pu'er* tea is regarded as the Oriental "drinkable marvel."

Talking about *pu'er* tea cannot be done without talking about the ancient roads of tea and horses, zigzagging along the Hengduan Mountains in southeast China. It was on these ancient roads by which *pu'er* tea had been carried to distant lands all over the world. The north road leads to many inland provinces via Kunming and it was on this road that the tribute tea to the Emperor had been carried to Beijing through express delivery. The northwest road leads to Tibet via Dali, Lijiang and Zhongdian, and from Lhasa extends to Nepal and India and so on. There are three southern roads, respectively, the east leading to Vietnam, the south leading to Laos and the southwest leading to Myanmar and Thailand. The horses travelled to and fro in an endless stream. There were far more than cakes of air-dried *pu'er* tea in what they were delivering. On their backs were also the mystical sights, the legendary fate of the people and their pious beliefs, as well as their soul-stirring history.

The Unique Fragrance of Scented Tea

As the name "scented tea" implies, it is a tea that is mixed with flowers. But different from beautifying tea, which is composed of pure, dried flowers, and is a current trend among girls and young ladies, the perfume of the flowers from the tea can only be smelled, but the flowers are invisible. Scented tea is done by reprocessing the tea, which includes adding

Beautiful and elegant jasmine flowers.

dried, scented flowers so as to mix the two types of scent. By doing so, the scented tea possesses both the pleasant freshness of the tea and the strong scent of the flowers. Scented tea is also known as "flower-smoked tea," "fragrant flower tea" or *xiangpian*.

The tea leaves for scented tea mainly come from green tea. Sometimes black tea leaves and oolong tea leaves are also used. Among the different kinds of green tea, the baked, dark green tea is the most suitable for making scented tea. There are varieties of fragrant flowers that are appropriate for making scented tea, with jasmine ranking first. The others include gardenia flowers, *zhulan* flower, roses, and *osmanthus* flowers. Gardenia-scented tea tastes strong and mellow; *zhulan*-scented tea, profound; rose-scented tea, pleasantly sweet; and *osmanthus*-scented tea, refreshing. Rose and black tea, which are both red, are a perfect match, while *osmanthus* goes well with oolong tea, with the former being strong-scented and the latter, light-scented. Of course, it is only natural that ingenious concepts are sure to produce unique tastes.

Jasmine tea fully deserves the honor of queen of different kinds of scented tea. Jasmine has a noble, unsullied character and is pleasantly fragrant. It breaks out into blossom in hot summer and sends forth perfume at night. When the jasmine flowers are about to bloom, a large amount of jasmine buds that are ready to burst are collected. At nightfall when the buds are half open and sending forth strong fragrance, they are mixed with tea leaves; this process is called "mixing the buds with tea leaves." The jasmine buds are taken from the tea leaves after the fragrance is spent and the buds have withered; this process is called "removing the buds." The jasmine buds are usually put into the tea leaves group by group and the fragrance seeps into the tea time after time. When this is done, the buds are removed from the tea. Ordinary

Fine teacups with caps convey the refined and graceful taste of the tea-drinkers.

jasmine tea needs "mixing" once and one "removing," "mixing" twice and one "removing," or "mixing" three times and one "removing." But extraordinary jasmine tea needs "mixing" four times and one "removing," "mixing" five times and one "removing" or even "mixing" six times and one "removing."

Jasmine tea is produced in Fujian, Guangdong, Suzhou, Zhejiang and Sichuan Provinces. The jasmine tea produced in Fujian enjoys the greatest reputation. Apart from using baked, dark green tea leaves to make jasmine tea, people from Fujian also use *longjing*, *biluochun*, silver needles and *maofeng* to make jasmine tea. There are numerous famous brands with these types of jasmine tea. The well-known Select Fujian Jasmine *Dabaihao* is made by mixing the *Dabaicha* young tea-leaf shoots produced in Fuding in early spring as the tea leaves with the single-petal and double-petal jasmine bud alternately, and the production process undergoes seven "mixings" and one "removing." The jasmine tea produced in Suzhou also enjoys a great reputation. Jasmine can be seen everywhere around Huqiu. If you're visiting Suzhou on a summer night and happen to hear the sound of the bell coming from the outskirts of the city, never forget that the jasmine is breaking out into blossom at that moment and the soul of the flowers has found her home in the charms of tea. What an effervescent fragrance it will be!

Chrysanthemum Blossom and Other Flowers Used in Making Tea

In the golden autumn of October, the chrysanthemum breaks out into full blossom. It is a pleasure of life to enjoy the wonderful view of the chrysanthemum blossom while eating crabs. Moreover, the chrysanthemum blossom is not only a wonderful delight to the eyes, but it is also drinkable. Autumn is also the season for tea workers to collect the chrysanthemum blossom and make tea. According to *Compendium of Materia Medica*, a work about Chinese medicine written by Li Shizhen in 1578, the chrysanthemum blossom tastes sweet and cool and is effective in relieving internal heat and calming the liver to improve eyesight. The chrysanthemum blossom mentioned in *Compendium of Materia Medica* does not refer to the decorative chrysanthemum blossom usually seen, but refers only to the white chrysanthemum blossom, which can be used as

In traditional Chinese culture, chrysanthemum is a symbol of noble and stainless personality and refined and graceful character.

Chinese medicine as well as for tea making.

Appearing fine, elegant and pure white, the chrysanthemum blossom emits a faint, sweet fragrance that flows into the heart. When placed into boiled water, chrysanthemum blossom tea tastes pleasantly sweet and fragrant with a slight bitterness. Drinking chrysanthemum blossom tea in spring is effective in curing dampness-induced diseases; in summer, relieving summer heat; in autumn, relieving internal heat; and in winter, moistening the lungs, skin, etc. The Chinese believe that drinking chrysanthemum blossom teas constantly can relieve internal heat and improve eyesight, supplement energy and enhance beauty, regulate the stomach and the spleen and prolong life.

At the end of each October, all the chrysanthemums come into full bloom, such as the Hangbai chrysanthemum in Tongxiang of Zhejiang, Huangshan Gong chrysanthemum on the Huangshan Mountain, Bo chrysanthemum in Bozhou, Chu chrysanthemum in Chuzhou of Anhui, Chuan chrysanthemum in Zhongjiang of Sichuan and De chrysanthemum in Deqing of Zhejiang. Of all these kinds of chrysanthemum, the

Chrysanthemum scented tea has a unique medicinal effect.

Hangbai chrysanthemum and the Gong chrysanthemum on the Huangshan Mountain are the best loved among the people. The Gong chrysanthemum, grown among the sea of mists on the Huangshan Mountain and drawing the miraculous power from heaven and earth, mountains and rivers and the clouds and mists, is exceedingly precious. The Hangbai chrysanthemum, grown in the homeland of fish, rice and silkworm culture in south China, is one of the eight traditional Chinese medicinal herbs for export in Zhejiang. The Hangbai chrysanthemum can be collected about five times each year and all the Hangbai chrysanthemum blossom picked at the first time is full and of the same size. The tea made with it tastes pleasantly sweet and fragrant. It is also a rare treasure.

Glass tea utensils are best for drinking chrysanthemum tea, because chrysanthemum blossom tea not only serves to make you feel refreshed, it also moistens the throat and is pleasing to both the eye and the mind. When put in boiled water, the air-dried chrysanthemum blossom seems to awaken from its long sleep. Unfurling quietly, the petals begin to dance gracefully and, bit by bit, the splendor of life bursts out again. The tea made with the chrysanthemum blossom appears light yellow, clear and bright. The petals in the water appear jade white and the pistils and stamens bright yellow, waving in the water, which forms a scene of dazzling beauty. Chrysanthemum can be also added into tea, mulberry leaves and Chinese hawthorn. These drinks have the medicinal effect of relieving internal fever, lowering the blood pressure, and eliminating tension and indigestion.

Apart from the chrysanthemum blossom tea, which is familiar to all people, nearly all the herbal flowers can be used as tea in China. Roses can regulate *qi* energy and improve blood circulation; narcissus can help the hair grow black and moisten the skin; pot marigold excels in nourishing the liver and improving eyesight; magnolia can tone up the heart and calm the nerves; mint can reduce the bloated stomach and Roselle can reduce

freckles and enhance beauty. Moreover, honeysuckles and sterculia seeds are effective in relieving internal heat; Gynostemma-herb can help bring down blood pressure and *momordica grosvenori* can relieve inflammation. These cannot only serve as daily drinks, but they've already been included in the prescriptions of traditional Chinese medicine. All women love herbal-flower drinks, not only for the rich, sweet scent, but also for their inherent medicinal effects. Have herbal-flower drinks, and, definitely, you'll be a beauty.

All types of flower-scented tea are available on the market.

Even Plain Water May Have the Scent of Tea in a Yixing Red Porcelain Teapot

Chinese people have always placed much emphasis on "opportune time, advantageous terrain and popular support" when they want to accomplish something. There are also three basic requirements in enjoying a cup of good tea, "select tea, quality water and wonderful tea utensils." Naturally, top-quality tea is a must. The water for making tea should also be given special attention, for instance, *longjing* tea must go with the fountain from Hupao, and only by doing so can they be a perfect match. Besides select tea and quality water, a wonderful teapot is also needed, on that will be worthy of the sweet scent of the tea and the bright, clear water.

Yixing, Jiangsu Province, known as "Yangxian" in ancient times, is located on the west side of the Taihu Lake. As an old saying goes, "Take no pearls and jewels from this world of ours. How could they be placed on a bar with a handful of soil from Yangxian?" This handful of soil, which is considered more precious than pearls and jewels, is the red soil used to make red porcelainware. Red porcelain teapot is made of this red soil and

Quality red-porcelain tea utensils can well preserve the color, scent and flavor of the tea for a considerably longer time.

has long been a must in the collection of tea drinkers.

Red-porcelain teapots in different shapes.

Unlike glasses, which are sparkling and crystal clear, and chinaware, which is smooth and delicate, red porcelainware is of primitive simplicity and elegance, unadorned and reserved, which tallies with the way of cultivating personal moral character practiced by learned men in China. The art of red porcelain, which consists of plastic arts, poetry, calligraphy, painting, seal-carving and sculpture, is a manifestation of the overall quality of the Chinese literati. Throughout the ages these men shared a strong love for red porcelain. They were also keen on placing their literary grace and personal interests in the small, red, porcelain teapots. The sentimental Chinese men are profuse in their praise of red porcelain teapots, saying they are "as gentle as gentlemen, as bold and uninhibited as men, as romantic as poets, as graceful as beauties, as profound as recluses, as free and unconventional as youths, as elegant as fairy maidens and as honest and clean as hermits."

Comments on red porcelain teapots rest with the following five aspects, "soil, shape, technology, inscriptions and use." Soil refers to the red soil from Yixing. Rich in iron, plastic, cold-resistant and high-temperature resistant, the red soil does not overshadow the tea's scent and it preserves the original taste. The shapes of the red porcelain teapots are varied, which accords with the saying, "Though square-shaped, each is different from the other; though round-shaped, each is different from the other." Red porcelain teapots can be also divided into several other kinds of shapes, such as natural, geometrical, muscle- and horizontal, or they

A Yixing red porcelain teapot from the Qing Dynasty.

can be classified into long-necked teacups, short-necked teacups and handle-on-top teapots. Also, red porcelain teapots can be divided into the type that has no patterns and the type that has patterns. There are no fixed rules to the classification of the shapes. What's good or bad in a teapot is totally subjective. However, the one factor that is readily responded to is a good teapot. The traditional technology of teapot making is molding by hand; first, the body; then, the lower part; next, the main part; and, finally, the handle, the mouth and the lid. The molding of each part, like the composition of points, lines and surface, as well as harmony and tightness, must be handled with meticulous care. The inscriptions on a teapot, whether a poem, handwriting, painting or a seal, can make a good teapot even better, or give it a tremendous boost in value. The criteria for a good teapot comprise proper volume, moderate height, tight lid and smooth water flow. The "first-hand teapot" that can make four cups of tea is often used as the "pouring pot" in a kung fu tea set. In addition, tall teapots are good for black tea and short teapots are good for green tea. The tea will lose its original taste and flavor if it's steeped in the wrong teapot.

A top-quality red porcelain teapot demands not only connoisseurship, but also maintenance. It is advisable to use one teapot for one type of tea only, and only by doing so can the tea scent last and smell pure and perfect. New teapots should be boiled in tea so as to eliminate the smell of smoke and earth before they are used. Before tea is made, the teapot is warmed with hot water first. When the tea is finished, the dregs and residue are emptied, and the teapot is rinsed inside and out and then dried in the shade. Red porcelain teapots need frequent cleaning. In addition, they especially need to be rubbed by hands so as to make them smooth and full. Teapot maintenance, similar to moral character cultivation, attaches great importance to calmness and tranquility of body and mind as well as perseverance. Even plain water, when added to a matured, red porcelain teapot, may have the scent of tea.

Kung Fu Tea

The term "kung fu tea" is not the name of a certain kind of tea, but actually refers to the ceremonies related to making tea and acquiring, sipping or savoring tea. For the Chinese people, tea is drunk not solely for the purpose of satisfying thirst; they also drink it to savor its taste and delight in the pleasant flavor of the tea. This has resulted in the emergence of the "living fossil of tea ceremony"—kung fu tea—which places more emphasis on savoring and enjoying its flavor than on tea drinking itself.

Kung fu tea is very popular among the people living in the regions of Chaozhou and Shantou of Guangdong as well as Zhangzhou and Quanzhou of Fujian.

Kung fu tea sets are common in every family in Chaozhou and Shantou.

Generally, kung fu tea is made with oolong tea leaves. The rich flavor of oolong tea leaves matches well with the implication of the term "kung fu." The oolong tea leaf is tender and green in the center and dark brown on the rim, which looks wonderful. The partial-fermenting processing technology of oolong tea, which lies between that of black tea and green tea, imbues oolong tea both with the strong, sweet flavor of black tea and the pleasant scent of green tea. The color of the oolong tea made in this way appears clear, bright and yellow, as if tempered with the red and green on a palette. Mild in quality, oolong tea is neither cold nor warm.

The tea set for making kung fu tea may be simple or complex. A full tea set may include over a dozen pieces, such as the tin can that is used to contain tea, the porcelain pot that is used to boil water, the pouring pot for pouring the tea, teacups, as well as articles for rinsing, tea tray, tea saucer, towels and so on. The porcelain pot that is used to boil water is made of red soil and the lid of the pot will dance continuously when the water is boiling hot. The pots for pouring the tea, which are made from the red porcelain from Yixing, are considered the best. Teapots and teacups should be small in size and shallow so as to accumulate and keep the flavor and fragrance of the tea. The water from the mountains is regarded as the best water for making tea; the river water, of medium quality; and the water from wells, inferior. The best fire used to boil the water is an active charcoal fire with flames.

Three or four is the best number for the amount of people drinking kung fu tea together. One person drinking solo will feel lonely and too many drinking together will result in cacophony. The normal practice is that the host prepares the tea. The pot for boiling water is placed over a small, red porcelain stove. The water is boiled, using a feather fan to fan the stove and steel rod to stir the charcoal. When the water starts boiling, the boiling water is poured onto the pouring teapot and teacups to warm them. The tea leaves are arranged onto

When making tea, pour boiling water from a high point so as to cool down the water.

a piece of paper and the thick leaves are separated from the thin ones. The thick tea leaves are placed on the bottom and around the outlet of the teapot, the tea flakes in the middle part and the others over the surface of the tea. This process is known as "receiving tea." The teapot should not be filled to excess. When the water in the boiling pot boils again, the boiling water is poured into the teapot around its opening from a higher point. As the tea flakes rise to the surface of the water, it is removed with the lid. The lid is replaced on the teapot and then hot water is poured over the teapot so as to have the scent

Making friends through tea-drinking is a pleasure.

accumulate in the teapot. This being done, the teacups are warmed and the tea is poured from the teapot, which should be held at a lower point. The tea should never be poured into the teacups one after another. The teapot is moved to and fro over the teacups and the tea is poured evenly into the cups. By doing so, the color, scent and flavor of the tea in different cups will be exactly the same.

When enjoying kung fu tea, first its fragrance must be smelled and then its color, appreciated. After being drunk, the faint sweet scent of the tea from the bottom of the teacup can still be smelled. Ardent tea lovers even smell the bottom of the teacup three times after they finish drinking. Kung fu tea is strong and contains a hardy base. The first cup tastes bitter, but after several rounds of drinking and talking, the drinkers are enveloped in a quiet, amiable and leisurely mood. This is called "kung fu." Drinking kung fu tea is a full reflection of the spirit of tea art special to the Chinese people, represented by the concept of upholding nature and being free and unrestrained. It also displays the human kindness particular to the Chinese people—kindhearted, honest, reserved and profound in thought.

In the regions of Chaozhou and Shaotou, each household has a kung fu tea set, and people from Chaozhou and Shantou need to have a few cups of tea every day. They entertain their guests or friends with tea. Also, they have kung fu tea to accompany Chaozhou-style dishes. Chaozhou people call tea, "tea rice." They need to drink tea after they rise in the morning. They won't go without tea even for one day. Obviously, they are attached to their tea and view it as an integral part of their lives. Chaozhou people never give up kung fu tea, even when they go to foreign countries or leave their hometowns. Therefore, where there are Chaozhou people, there are the living relics of the Chinese tea art. Those who sip and enjoy kung fu tea definitely will feel the loyal hearts of tea lovers.

Tea Drinking among China's 55 Ethnic Groups

China is a multinational country with numerous traditions and customs. All the people from each of the 55 ethnic groups are tea drinkers. The tea that is popular in one ethnic group usually differs from another, according to local conditions and circumstances or time of growth and preservation. Each has its own unique quality marked by the differences between the local customs, psychology and temperament of various nationalities.

The Tibetans live on the "roof of the world," where the air is thin and the weather is cold. Vegetables do not grow well in Tibet, but here tea can be perfectly preserved. Drawing nourishment from tea, the Tibetans invented the unique buttered tea. Butter is the solid, yellow fat on the surface of boiled cow milk when it has

An aged man stir-frying tea.

cooled. The tea is the pressed brick tea. First, the brick tea is broken into pieces, boiled in water and then tea is made; the tea is poured into a bamboo or long, wooden, round tube. Following this, butter and salt are added into the tube. Prepared, fried, crushed walnut meat, peanuts, sesame and pine nuts, according to different individual taste, are also added. The stuffing is beaten in the tube with a special wooden pestle until the tea and the various condiments are well-mixed. This done, the buttered tea is ready. Buttered tea, salty with a slight sweetness and fragrance, is a treasure that Tibetans use to entertain guests and friends. When drinking buttered tea at a Tibetan's home, do not drink it in one gulp. Instead, the teacup will be filled continuously as you drink. The Tibetan host will keep pouring tea with eager attentiveness, so the tea in the cup remains full.

The Inner Mongolian pasture abounds in milk products. Generation after generation, the Mongolians have been keen on drinking salty milk tea made from cooked brick tea. The first thing the industrious Mongolian housewives do after they get out of bed is making milk tea. Water is boiled in an iron pot, then broken brick tea is added, and when the tea is boiled, salt, butter, a spoonful of milk skin and a bowl of fresh milk are added in succession. Soon, the salty, fragrant flavor of the milk tea fills the yurt. This pot of milk tea is placed over a slow fire and the whole family drinks it all day. The Mongolians have three tea meals and one regular meal. They have the regular meal in the evening after their return from the pasture. However, milk tea is always ready and absolutely indispensable.

The "three-course tea" popular among the Bai ethnic group is a manifestation of the art of serving tea, as well as a portrayal of the charm of life. First, the porcelain teapot for cooking tea is placed over the fire. As the host chats with his guests, he puts tea into the porcelain teapot while it's getting warmed, and then shakes the teapot gently. When the tea leaves begin to turn yellow, boiling water is poured into the teapot. When a sizzling

A Tibetan woman is making buttered tea.

sound can be heard coming from the teapot, tea flakes emerge from the water, and the "thunder tea" is ready. When the tea appears amber, it is ready to serve to the guest. The tea served at the first round tastes bitter, so it is called "bitter tea." At the second round, walnut pieces, sesame and brown sugar are added, so it is called "sweet tea." At the third round, toasted cheese and honey are added, cinnamon bark, pop rice and Chinese prickly ash are also added, and thus it has the five flavors of sweet, sour, bitter, pungent and salty. The tea served at the third round is called "aftertaste tea." Bitterness comes first, then comes sweetness and, finally, aftertaste. Thus, the people from the Bai ethnic group offer a striking expression of their understanding of life through tea drinking.

A teacup used by the people of the Hui ethnic group, commonly known as "*Sanpaotai*," consists of three parts, the cap, the cup and the saucer. Added in the tea are white sugar, brown sugar, dates, walnut meat, dried *longan* pulp, sesame, raisin, and fruit of Chinese wolfberry, all of which benefit the mind and health. When drinking tea, people from the Hui ethnic group do not lift up the cap of the teacup. They must scrape off the tea leaves with the cap before drinking. The more the leaves are scraped by the cap, the better the tea will be. People from the Hui ethnic group are extremely fond of "*Sanpaotai*." Gifts exchanged at young couple's engagement ceremonies are all related to tea. So the term engagement is also called "*Dingcha*" ("tea engagement").

Oil tea of the Dong ethnic group is made by stir-frying and cooking tea leaves and rice. When eating oil tea, people of the Dong ethnic group add popped rice, soybean, peanuts, pig liver, and stuffed dumplings made of sticky rice flour. Bamboo-tube fragrant tea of the Dai ethnic group is made by putting the tea leaves into tender bamboo tubes and roasting them. When the bamboo tube turns to yellow from green, the bamboo tube is split and the toasted tea leaves are ready for making tea. The Lei tea popular in the Tujia ethnic group is made by grinding and cooking the newly picked tea leaves, ginger and husked rice together. The sweet tea of the Zhuang ethnic group is made by cooking the leaves of wild shrubs. When a young man from the Zhuang ethnic group pays a visit to seek a marriage union, the girl offers sweet tea. If the tea contains sugar, it implies that the girl has fallen in love with the young man in her heart. In addition, the Uygurs drink milk skin tea, the people from the Korean ethnic group drink ginseng tea, the Hanis drink iron-pot tea, the Naxis drink salt tea, the Buyei ethnic people drink green tea, the Gaoshan ethnic people drink mandarin orange tea, the Jingpo ethnic people drink pickled tea,

A young girl of the Bai ethnic group is making tea.

and the Dulong ethnic people drink stewed tea... The different tea flavors, the tea fragrances, the art of serving tea and the tea ceremonies of all nationalities in China—with life in the yurts, on the flatlands in southwest China, in the mountain villages and the two-storey, bamboo-stilt houses—await your presence.

DRINK AND WINE CULTURE

National Drink Intoxicates the World

Grain production has dominated people's lives in China, a traditionally agricultural country with a 5,000-year history of farming. Made from grain and viewed as its essence, wine runs in the blood of this nation. The Chinese, from the highest as kings and emperors to the humblest as soldiers and peddlers, have always respected and loved wine. With wine, kings worship heaven, commoners express feelings, writers find inspiration, warriors discover courage, boys transform into men and women acquire charm. Wine has enveloped society so completely that no-one can escape it, in life or death. It is a major ingredient in life today—in conveying hope, in expressing wishes and in bonding with others.

Moutai wine that enjoys an international reputation.

The two main types of Chinese wine are *baijiu* (literally "white wine"), a strong, colorless liquor and *huangjiu* (literally "yellow wine"), a golden-brown rice wine. *Baijiu* includes a few varieties, such as the moutai-flavored *Moutai* wine of Guizhou, strong-flavored *Luzhoulaojiao* of Sichuan, light-flavored *Fenjiu* of Shanxi, rice-flavored *Sanhuajiu* of Guangxi and multi-flavored *Dongjiu* of Guizhou.

Moutai wine has a 2,000-year legacy. As early as 135

Moutai Town in Guizhou —a distant view of the hometown of *Moutai* wine.

BC, Emperor Wudi of the Western Han Dynasty marveled at *Goujiangjiu* being produced in the town of Maotai, Guizhou Province, in southwest China. Chinese officials took *Moutai* wine to the Panama-Pacific Exposition in 1915. Because the bottles were black without clear, distinct labels, visitors at the expo walked past the exhibition without noticing them. One of the Chinese officials became so frustrated at this that he smashed one of the bottles on the floor. The bottle shattered, the content's extraordinary odor saturated the air and people were drawn to it. Later, *Moutai* wine was awarded the golden medal and became internationally recognized.

Moutai wine is named after its place of origin. With beautiful scenery, moderate weather, clear waters and rich soil, the small town produces a special sorghum and microorganisms that are indispensable to the brewing process. *Moutai* wine can only be produced in Maotai town and no other location would be suitable, because the fermentation process is long, complicated and seasonal. It has to be fermented eight times, distilled nine times, both at a very high temperature, and aged in a cellar for three years before it can be blended. The finished product tastes mellow and smooth, and has a lingering flavor without the side effect of a burning throat or aching stomach. With *Moutai* wine, you can have several more cups than you normally would, for you are not likely to get drunk, and

The age-old and
mysterious wine cellar
of *Moutai* wine.

it is not as harsh to the liver as other liquors can be.

A wine with artistic, cultural and historical flavor, *Moutai* wine has witnessed the birth and growth of the People's Republic of China. It became the drink for the state banquet at the 1949 national foundation ceremony. When the new China made its first appearance on the world stage at the 1954 Geneva International Conference, *Moutai* wine was served to foreign representatives and journalists. Many political figures have tasted *Moutai* wine in China. One of the most popular legends about *Moutai* wine is "Fire in the White House." Premier Zhou Enlai once showed President Nixon how liquor could be set aflame. Nixon was fascinated with the trick and took two bottles of *Moutai* wine back to the United States. At home in the White House, Nixon tried to impress his wife and daughter with the same trick. Unfortunately, the bowl that contained the liquor heated up and cracked, setting the tablecloth on fire, and alarms were set off. "You almost burned down the White House!" Kissinger later joked with Deng Xiaoping. As a "star" at national banquets and a state gift for foreign leaders for over half a century, *Moutai* wine has played a big part in China's diplomatic affairs. It is the Chinese national drink that intoxicates the world.

Huangjiu—Chinese Character Matured with Age

*H*uangjiu (golden-brown rice wine), is indigenous to China; *huangjiu*, wine and beer comprise the three ancient drinks in the world. Just as vodka is to Russia and sake is to Japan, so *huangjiu* is to China; it belongs to the group of extraordinary items that make this nation unique.

Confucianism teaches people to practice the golden mean or the middle way, as neither "more" nor "less" is perfect. *Huangjiu* is such an ideal. It tastes neither so strong as liquor nor so flat as beer. The Chinese celebrate harmony, with the hope that everything in the universe can coexist peacefully. As a perfect mixture of six flavors—the sweetness and sourness of wine, the bitterness and hotness of liquor and the freshness and astringency of beer—*huangjiu* represents the natural balance between extremes.

Huangjiu has several varieties, including *Laojiu* of Fuji-

A wine worker at work.

an, *Fenggangjiu* of Jiujiang, *Huiquanjiu* of Wuxi, *Zhenzhuhongjiu* of Guangdong, *Lanlingmeijiu* of Shandong, *Laojiu* of Shanghai and *Huangjiu* of Dalian, none of which have achieved the status of Shaoxing *Huangjiu*, which is synonymous with Chinese *huangjiu*. Shaoxing *Huangjiu* owes its success to the fine water flowing down Mount Kuaiji, along with the sediment that settles before flowing into Lake Jian. Premium-white glutinous rice and high-quality wheat, mixed with this magical water, transform into a sweet, pure, redolent and mellow drink, the one and only Shaoxing *Huangjiu*.

Upper: Shaoxing Winery.

Lower: The outside of Shaoxing yellow wine jars are painted with a coat of lime before they are sealed up.

Shaoxing *Huangjiu* is categorized according to its sweetness. *Zhuangyuanhong*, the least sweet, is a classic, dry wine. The most famous kind of *huangjiu* is *Jiafan*, and the aged *Jiafan* kept in jars is called *Huadiao*, named after the colorful embossing on the jugs containing it. And *Nü'erhong* (literally "daughterly red") is the most beautiful. Legend goes

Three boatmen drinking yellow wine by the river in Shaoxing.

that a tailor in Shaoxing made several jugs of good wine when his wife was pregnant, expecting to serve it to families and friends when his "son" was born. As the woman gave birth to a daughter, the tailor got so mad that he buried the wine in the yard under a tree. Eighteen years later, the baby girl grew into a beautiful and intelligent young woman, a gem to her father. On the day she was married, the tailor dug up the wine and opened a jar. Out wafted a potent fragrance, and the wine was a deep-red color; hence, the name "*Nü'erhong*," which literally means "daughterly red." Since then, every local household has followed suit, making several jugs of good wine when a baby girl is born, not opening them until the girl marries and begins her own life. Later, people made wine when a boy was born, too, hoping that he would place first in the highest imperial exam (zhuangyuan); hence, the name "*Zhuangyuanhong*."

Wine Cultures of Ethnic Groups

Chinese ethnic groups, except Muslims who do not drink, mostly love wine and are good at producing it. They believe that it is inhospitable not to serve some. Different ethnicities have different kinds of wine and drinking customs.

The Mongolians traditionally make wine with horse milk. The wine season lasts from mid-summer until early autumn every year, when a lovely fragrance fills every tent, and celebratory songs and dances are performed at every family gathering or holiday banquet. The Mongolians regard wine as the essence of food. When they propose a toast, they usually invite the guest to drink three cups of wine with them in one go. Nothing pleases the host more than having an inebriated guest. Without great tolerance for liquor, do not enter a drinking contest with the Mongolians.

Tibetan wine is brewed from highland barley. The strongest can be of over 60 percent vol. In a Tibetan home, a guest should finish a cup of wine in three mouthfuls: first, the guest has a sip, and the host fills the cup; then the guest has another sip before the host fills the cup again; finally the guest tosses the cup. If the guest is not good at drinking liquor, he should dip the third finger of his right hand into the wine and tap it away into the air, a gesture of respect to the heavens, the earth, gods, families and friends, and the host will take this cue to not insist anymore.

The Yi people living in Sichuan produce wine from bitter buckwheat, corn and potatoes. When it is served, the first cup is offered to the gods and the second to the elders before everyone shares the rest. The "guest wine" of the Naxi people is made from grain sorghum, barley and wheat. As its name suggests, it is served to the guest, but also kept for a newborn baby girl, like *"Nü'erhong."* The Dulong people mix rice, wheat or grain sorghum with herb wine and place it in bamboo tubes. Everyone

Wine is always indispensable on
happy occasions.

can drink from the tube when it is ripe. The Shui people put pig bile into rice wine and serve it to guests, meaning that they share good fortune and bad times. The Tujia people have "sweet wine tea," which is actually a wine made from glutinous rice or grain sorghum, and mix it with honey and spring water. The Korean people make the "yearly wine" with rice as a basic material, and also with balloon flower, fangfeng, prickly ash, cinnamon and other Chinese herbs. The drink is served during Spring Festival to pray for longevity and ward away evil. The Hani people steep popcorn made from newly harvested corn into their wine to make "new corn wine," as a celebration for a bumper crop.

Different ethnic groups have different wine cultures. The Miao people have "on-the-way wine," which is served to guests on their way to the host's place. The Lisu people sprinkle wine onto the ground, showing respect to their ancestors, and then take one sip themselves as a gesture of goodwill before offering it to guests. The Zhuang people offer guests wine in a spoon instead of a cup. The Wa people give a section of bamboo with wine to a guest, who then returns it to the host, who sips it before the guest finishes it. The Yi people are the most wonderful: everyone sits on the ground—guests as well as hosts—as a cup of wine passes from one to another, as though everyone is family.

Drinking Etiquette

T he Chinese have their unique wine culture. Confucianism emphasizes a moral code, and it is considered a virtue to offer wine to the heavens, gods, the elderly and guests. As too much drinking harms one's health and job as well, the Chinese believe that one should drink half as much as one actually can; this corresponds to the philosophy of the golden mean.

One should also drink with decorum. In the old days, the juniors had to defer and get permission from the seniors before they could drink. As long as there was wine in the senior's cup, the junior could not empty his. The host had to stand up to toast guests, who would reciprocate. When toasting someone, the toaster could drink three cups at most, and the toaster had to toss his or her cup as a gesture of sincerity. Some of these customs are still alive today. Everyone has his own place at a banquet, ensuring that it is a happy gathering.

The Chinese drink on numerous occasions and give different names to these wine parties (*jiu*), such as the new-year-feast for Spring Festival, the Pure Brightness Festival on Tomb-Sweeping Day, the Chinese Valentine feast on the seventh evening of the seventh moon, the family reunion feast on the Mid-Autumn Festival, the chrysanthemum feast on the Double Ninth Festival, the mid-winter feast around December 22, and the Tusu feast on the first day of the lunar year. The fragrance of wine imbues social life. A newborn baby certainly makes a good occasion for celebration. People drink when the child is three days old (*sanzhaojiu*), one month old (*manyuejiu*),

"Having drunk one *dou* of wine, Li Bai produces one hundred poems." Ever since antiquity, wine, poetry and men of letters have been closely associated with one another.

115

one hundred days old (*bairijiu*) and one year old (*dezhoujiu*). There are also feasts on birthdays, weddings and funerals. Moreover, banquets are held when a house is built (*shangliangjiu*), when someone has a new home (*xinjujiu*), when a visitor from afar arrives (*jiefengjiu*), and when family or friends leave (*jianxingjiu*). Farmers have banquets when setting out rice plants (*chayangjiu*) and after a harvest (*fengshoujiu*), merchants celebrate when opening a new business (*kaizhangjiu*) or cashing dividends (*fenhongjiu*) and soldiers have banquets before being sent to the battlefield (*chushijiu*) and after returning victoriously (*qinggongjiu*). For the Chinese, wine is a divine gift. No wine, no party.

Night Banquet of Han Xizai (detail), by Gu Hongzhong of the Five Dynasties period, gives us a lifelike portrayal of wine-drinking in ancient China.

The object of these feasts is not to eat and drink, but to join in merrymaking. Using wine as penalty, a great variety of wine games have arisen. In the old days, the refined class would have poetry contests when drinking, while common people liked to play "guessing fingers," in which each party held up a number of fingers simultaneously with his opponent and shouted out the number that he guessed would be held up by both parties. Some of these games are still played today.

The Oriental Charms of Wine Bars

Bars, though an exotic civilization, have taken on a brand-new appearance in China which boasts a long history of liquor culture. Today, it has become an indispensable part of life for the fashion people to hang out in bars. The alienated term "hanging out" implies kind of leisure and comfort, a sense of satisfaction, some languid and even an element of degeneration.

There are more bars in Beijing than in any other city in China. The various kinds of bars in Beijing, ranging from 20 to 600 square meters in size, vary equally dramatically in theme and flavor. When night falls, the city's white-collar employees, intellectuals, professionals, artists, music lovers, college students and other people with leisure time would habitually swarm in these bars. They may dance to their hearts' content in groups to the beat of rock & roll music, or chat softly in twos and threes over cups of wine. A sub-cultural zone, with the young social elites as its core, has thus taken shape and evolved in the bars.

In the 1990s, two young students who returned home from Japan after accomplishing their studies there set up Beijing's first bar in the foreigner-populated embassy

To attract the attention of the customers, the supermarket offers a good supply of wine of various brand names.

district. At that time, bars were frequented only by foreigners, foreign students studying in China and a few people from the intellectual circles. However, bars have been quickly accepted by the Chinese people and integrated into the modern urban civilization of China. And the bar groups springing up around the embassy district have quickly snowballed into the well-known Sanlitun Bar Street. Today, while Sanlitun remains the most important place for night life in Beijing, more bars with more distinctive flavors have been mushrooming in every corner of the capital city.

The bars in Shichahai neighborhood have combined fashion with tradition: the mottled-bricked quadrangles blend in perfectly with the colorful cocktails. With the swaying lotus-shaped boats, the lamplight, the music, the drinkers will indulge themselves in the atmosphere even if the wine is not so intoxicating. The bar area in the vicinity of the Workers' Gymnasium is vibrant with of vitality and energy; the bar area round the Chaoyang Park is rational and quiet; the bar area close to the Factory 798 is a gathering place for a large circle of pioneer artists; facing the water, Yuandadu bar street is so quiet and peaceful as to remind us of the public houses far back in the Yuan Dynasty 800 years ago.

When bars first entered China, they were not only fashionable gathering places for the elite, but they also took on "native" features and thus became colorful as well. At present, most popular bars have distinctive

Bar rooms with distinctive styles are the places where numerous fashion young people meet.

themes. Among the theme bars, music bars account for the majority. There are a large number of talented singers in rock & roll bars, jazz bars, folk music bars. Besides these music bars, there are also other bars which have taken film, drawing, sculpture, collection, and cosplay, military issues, Chinese kung fu, and behavior art as their themes. Frequently visited by fashion people with the same interests, these bars have been stamped with the brands of fashionable Chinese culture.

Besides Beijing, other Chinese cities also have bars. The Maoming Road in Shanghai, Yanjiang Road in Guangzhou, Defu Lane in Xi'an, Nanshan Road in Hangzhou, West Jietang Road in Changsha, Shiquan Street in Suzhou, Sanjing Street in Shenyang, and Nanjing 1912 in Nanjing are all popular havens of bar culture. In such tourist destinations as Tibet, Yunnan and Guangxi, bar culture intermingles harmoniously with local ethnic cultural heritage, an example of miraculous combination of Western and Oriental cultures and customs.

Wine and liquor are of course the everlasting themes in all the bars. Among all the alcoholic drinks, beer tops the list of consumption volume in bars. In today's China, the main social force mainly represented by the 70s borns prefers beer to spirit. China has now become the second largest beer producer in the world, with many different brand names flourishing in different places: in the north, we have "Harbin," in the south, we have the "Pearl River," in the northwest, we have the "Yellow River," and in the southwest, we have "Chongqing." The traditional "Tsingtao Beer," with a history of more than 100 years, is deemed as the annals of the Chinese beer industry. And "Yanjing," as a new star, is the most popular beer in Beijing. People from Beijing would like to call the common Yanjing beer as "Pujing" (Putin) for short. Thus the name of our neighboring country's president can be heard frequently in restaurants.

Foreign tourists are drinking to their hearts' content at the Qingdao International Beer Festival.

Apart from the refreshing beer, exquisite cocktail, strong vodka, soft rum, and mellow whisky, red wine is also a most favored item for many wine lovers. The history of the Chinese red wine brewage can be dated back to the Western Han Dynasty (206 BC–AD 25) and the ancient Chinese red wine brewage reached its prime in the Tang Dynasty (618–907). "Fine grape wine in the evening-radiant cup," a famous line from Wang Han's poetic works, can serve as a proof for the development of China's wine industry achieved in ancient China. In the Ming Dynasty (1368–1644), Li Shizhen also mentioned some methods of wine making and the medicinal values of red wine several times in his *Compendium of Materia Medica*. Today, the Chinese wine industry is developing quickly. Such brand names as Zhangyu, Great Wall, and Dynasty etc., have become renowned names throughout the world. Breweries such as "Tonghua" in Jilin Province and "Mogao" in Gansu Province are producing icewine of superb quality which is generally regarded as typical luxury wine.

For people of present China, liquor or wine drinking serves not only as a trendy consumption, but also as a delight of life and a way of communication. It is something time-honored and trendy, traditional and open, and intimate and colorful.

ENTERTAINMENT

Folk Music Accompanying Social Life

O n the lunar New Year's Eve in 1998, in the golden halls of Vienna, the lively and magnificent *Radetzky March* was played with convention, and also with exotic flavor; it was the sound of nature from an ancient oriental civilization—an ensemble of Chinese traditional instruments. The West was enchanted by Chinese folk music, which has since travelled all over the world.

As the best accompaniment to social life, traditional Chinese music is played on various occasions such

"Twelve Girls Band" adds a modern vigor to ancient classical Chinese music.

as weddings, funerals and harvest festivals. Different instruments have different styles and convey different emotions. The percussions sound warm and spirited; the strings, melodious and elegant. *Sizhuyue* (the tunes performed on stringed and woodwind instruments), popular in Jiangsu and Zhejiang, are exquisite, while *Chuidayue* (those played on wind and percussion instruments), popular in Xi'an, are masculine.

Today, with pop music sweeping the world, traditional music still has numerous fans who are handing it down to younger generations. Famous pieces such as *Mei Hua San Nong* (*Three Variations of Plum Blossom*) played with bamboo flute, *Shi Mian Mai Fu* (*Ambush from All Sides*)

Urheen solo, *Jasmine*.

played with *pipa* (a plucked string instrument with a fretted fingerboard) and the ensemble *Chun Jiang Hua Yue Ye* (*Spring River on a Moonlit Night*) have been played and enjoyed for hundreds of years. Chinese parents often choose an traditional instrument for their children to learn to play, expecting music to open the door to traditional Chinese culture for them.

Music plays a crucial role in traditional operas and folk arts. For example, *wenchang* (civil scene) of the traditional opera is accompanied by a stringed instrument such as urheen, yu-kin and *sanxian* (a three-stringed plucked instrument), while *wuchang* (martial scene) is accompanied by percussive instruments such as drums and gongs. Amateurs usually cannot only sing but also play these instruments. In Chinese parks, visitors can often find energetic old men practicing opera singing with *jinhu* (a two-stringed instrument).

Local music troupes give traditional music another flavor. With simple and ordinary villagers as performers, these troupes are really of the people and for the people. The self-taught musicians play at weddings, funerals and

Ansai waist drum performance, majestic as high mountains and mighty rivers.

An aged man from the Loess Plateau playing *suona*.

important farming occasions such as the transplanting of rice seedlings and tea-leaf picking right in the field. Popular in north Shaanxi Province where almost every village has its own troupe and every family has one or two drummers, Ansai waist drum is a folk instrument with a powerful primitive charm. When the drums are beaten, the earth seems to tremble and the mountains seem to sway. Compared to the masculine instrument of the rugged loess plateau, *guzheng*, which is popular in the greenery of Jiangnan (south of the lower reaches of the Yangtze River) with mild weather, sounds elegant and sweet. The Moon Appreciating Evening on Mid-Autumn Day at the 24-bridge in Yangzhou, Jiangsu Province, features a *guzheng* ensemble.

Board Games

The leisure time of a scholarly Chinese gentleman has been largely occupied by the four arts of *Qin* (zither), *Qi* (board game), *Shu* (calligraphy) and *Hua* (painting), of which *Qin* shows a detachment from worldly desires, *Shu* and *Hua* are combined as an art form to represent the harmony between human and nature, while only *Qi* is played competitively. There are mainly two kinds of *Qi* in ancient China—go and chess. One is more like politics, which involves gambling and the power struggle of the aristocracy, while the other is more of a military game and is popular among the masses.

The earliest records of go date back to the Spring and Autumn Period (770–476 BC). The game starts on an empty board that contains a grid of 19 horizontal and vertical lines (simplified versions of the game can be played on a 9 x 9, 13 x 13 or 17 x 17 board) forming 361 intersections, a number running closely to the number of days in a year. The board is square while the stones are round, implying the ancient belief of "the square earth and the round sky." The stones are black or white, representing yin and yang. The nine points on the board are dotted and called "star points," corresponding to the nine stellar palaces from where the heavens are ruled, according to Chinese mythology. The point in the center is also known as the "central star," standing for the origin of the universe. The division of the go board into four quarters symbolizes the four seasons and the 90 intersections in each quadrant correspond to the days in every season. The shape of the board is a mysterious star map. The player with the black stones makes the first move. Both sides put stones on the crossings and the one who occupies the larger territory at the end wins. It appears to be a quiet and genteel game, but actually is highly competitive and exciting.

As an encounter of minds, go was called *duiyi* (chess play) or *shoutan* (hand conversation). It was a hobby of

A young Go "Master Player."

emperors who were good at strategic maneuvering and scholars who had refined taste. For example, Emperor Xuanzong in the Tang Dynasty and Emperor Taizong in the Song Dynasty were both go fans. They sought good players from all over the country, retained them in the court and provided special positions for them; thus *Guoshou* (national players) came into being. The historian Bangu from the Eastern Han Dynasty, the political figure Caocao in the Three Kingdoms Period, the litterateurs Fan Zhongyan, Ouyang Xiu, Sima Guang, Wang Anshi and Su Dongpo in the Northern Song Dynasty were all accomplished players.

Chinese chess (*xiangqi*) also has a long history difficult to trace. Compared to go, which was played in palaces and grand mansions, chess has always been more accessible. While the gentlemen fingered stones made of jade in their studies, peasants, craftsmen and peddlers enjoyed chess in the marketplace.

Chinese chess is played on a board of 9 x 10 points, and the board is divided in the middle by a "river." Each territory contains a king's palace of 3 x 3. There are 32 pieces in total, and the two sides are usually distinguished with red and black. The red moves first and the side that checkmates the opponent general wins. Both sides have 7 classes of pieces (General, Advisor, Elephant, Horse, Chariot, Cannon, and Pawn)

"Never regret your move in board games" is a rule strictly followed by board game players.

represented by Chinese characters. The General moves horizontally or vertically one unit at a time and cannot move out of the palace. The Advisor moves diagonally one unit at a time and cannot leave the palace, either. The Elephant moves exactly two points diagonally, not more or less. The Horse moves horizontally or vertically in any directions by one unit, then immediately follows with a move diagonally one unit towards the direction away from its original position. The Chariot moves horizontally or vertically in any direction by any number of units; the Cannon moves horizontally or vertically in any direction by any number of units, provided that it doesn't move through another piece. To capture a piece, a Cannon must jump over one piece that is between itself and its intended target. The Pawn moves forward one unit at a time. Having crossed over into enemy zone, it can also move left or right one unit at a time. It can never move backward.

Featured by strategy and tactics, go focuses on how to besiege the enemy. With head-to-head contests, Chinese chess emphasizes taking out the enemy pieces. While one is restrained and the other straightforward, both are highly competitive. Go is a game limited to a few people today. Out of over a billion people, only several hundred players rank at the national level; they compete with Japan and South Korea every year. As a loyal companion to ordinary people, Chinese chess is played everywhere, under a tree, in a park, often with an audience standing around. They may be total strangers to each other, the players as well as the onlookers, but a game can be enough to eliminate the distance and make them friends.

The Charm of Chinese Operas

It is performed in theaters, at teahouses, and in the open in the countryside. There are usually only a table and two chairs on the stage. The actors wear costumes and colorful makeup—white face stand for evil and treacherousness, red face loyalty and courage, black face an honesty and fiery temper. The performance breaks the limits of time and space in an imagined way. For example, raising a foot means going upstairs, stretching out both hands signifies opening a window, waving a whip implies riding a horse, and waving oars stands for rowing a boat. A fierce battle involving thousands of soldiers is represented by the wielding of spears, a trot around the stage means a journey of hundreds of miles, and a monologue brings a lapse of decades. Welcome to the world of traditional Chinese opera.

Almost every province in China has its unique form of opera. For example, Jiangsu has *Kunqu*, Shaanxi has *Qinqiang*, Zhejiang has *Yueju*, Hebei has *Bangzi*, and Anhui has *Huangmeixi*, among which Peking Opera is most the popular and influential. Traditional opera is a way of life as well as a form of art. It is still alive today, thanks to numerous amateurs and fans as well as professional actors.

The amateurs (*piaoyou*) refer to those opera fans who perform on stage when they are in the mood, just for entertainment and without any intention for material reward. There were quite a few famous amateurs in the old days, who were more accomplished than many

Different types of facial make-up in Peking Opera are vividly drawn, presenting bright gay colors as well as the loyal and upright and the wicked and treacherous.

professionals in the four aspects of *chang* (singing), *nian* (dialogue), *zuo* (acting) and *da* (martial arts). Some of them came from prestigious families and were very good at classical arts such as calligraphy, poetry, painting and music. They played not for a living but for fun; therefore, their performance was often more innovative and in better taste. The amateurs still play a crucial role in the world of opera today. Students and teachers sometimes play together in colleges and universities. Fans from different generations learn from each other in community cultural centers and children's centers. With *huqin* (a two-stringed Chinese violin), amateurs play and sing in parks, at teahouses, at street corners—actually anywhere convenient—and enjoy themselves. Even foreigners are charmed by traditional Chinese operas. They watch, listen and even learn to perform. Wearing makeup, putting on a costume, putting on a dramatic pose and striking up an aria... How Chinese!

There are many amateurs who love to give performances, and there are even more people having

Mu Guiying, brimming with energy and vitality, in Peking Opera The Women Generals from the Yang Family

Zhong Kui, a legendary deity in Chinese folklore who can exorcize evil spirits, is spitting fire in a local opera.

great fun just watching and listening. Once upon a time, you would invite your friend to a theater if you were really grand. Opposite the stage was a hall circled by balconies. There were table and stools in the hall, but the VIPs would go upstairs. It was expensive entertainment to watch an opera. You had to pay for the tea, the snacks, the hot towels as well as the tickets. Even shouting "bravo" was not free. The actors had to be awarded with cash. It was very noisy in the theatre, with the sound of gongs and drums and the waiters loudly greeting the customers. A real fan knew when to shout. A "bravo" at the wrong time would offend the actor as well as the other audience members. It was also a nasty trick to keep shouting "bravo," since the actor had to somersault or sing continuously until all the spectators stopped yelling.

Theaters are no longer exclusive realms of the rich, but the custom of sitting around a table and drinking tea while watching has been retained. Today, fans do not

Amateur performers of operas, happy and contented.

have to go to the theater to enjoy traditional operas, since they reach millions of people through modern media such as television. The first movie made in China is a recording of the Peking Opera *Battle of Mount Dingjun*, and the China Central Television (CCTV) has created a special channel for opera fans. During Spring Festival, almost every variety show on television includes traditional opera. The classic pieces have been recorded in CD and DVD for fans to enjoy at any time.

Folk Art Forms with Local Flavor

*S*huochang (talking and singing), the most direct way of expression, form a genre of popular entertainment that has existed in China for hundreds of years. There are *xiangsheng* (comic talk), *pingshu* (story-telling), *kuaiban* (clapper ballad), *dagu* (story telling accompanied at the dulcimer) and *errenzhuan* (a song-and-dance duet popular in Northeast China).

Regarded as a trick or sideshow to make people laugh, folk talking-and-singing had been struggling to survive. The entertainers performed at Tianqiao in Beijing, Confucian Temple in Nanjing, Baoguo Temple in Tianjin and the Temple of Town God in Shanghai. Since the founding of the People's Republic of China, these folk arts have been encouraged by the government and have left the marketplace to enter the state theatres.

It is said that there are about 400 forms of folk arts alive in China today, and *xiangsheng* (comic talk) is the most popular. As the prologue to many pieces of *xiangsheng* goes, "*xiangsheng* is a linguistic art, for which you have to be good at talking, imitating, teasing and singing," the entertainers must be versatile. It can be performed by one person (solo comic talk), two persons (comic dialogue) or a group of people (group cross-talk). Comic dialogue is the most common form of *xiangsheng*, with one person playing a leading role and the other supporting. The past several decades have seen a great number of famous artists and this form of entertainment has reached a wide audience. Many comic dialogue artists perform at teahouses and theaters in Beijing and Tianjin, where there are also large groups of fans.

Life is food for art, while art gives flavor back to life. Different natural environments produce different people and different forms of folk arts. *Pingshu* (story telling), popular in north China, is usually about historical legends and heroes. With a folding fan and a piece of wood to cue the audience, the entertainer takes the listeners to a world of fires, thunders, great strategists and chivalrous knights. It is usually performed serially, and the "to be continued" at the end of every installment never fails to tease the anxious fans. *Pingtan* is very popular in Jiangsu, Zhejiang and Shanghai. The performers play a three-stringed instrument or a lute and sing in Suzhou dialect, which sounds beautiful in a feminine way. Other forms of folk arts have their own features, too. *Shuanghuang* (a two-man act, with one speaking or singing while

A comic talk performance.

hiding behind the other who does the acting) is humorous, *danxianr* (story-telling to the accompaniment of two-stringed Chinese violin and drum) melodious, *Shandongkuaishu* (clapper ballad originated in Shandong Province) vivid, *jingyundagu* (story-telling in Beijing dialect with drum accompaniment) solemn and stirring, and *errenzhuan* (a song-and-dance duet popular in the northeast) lively and funny.

Suzhou *pingtan* (storytelling combined with ballad singing) is a typical folk art form of the folk arts in south China.

Wuqiao, Home of Acrobatics

Wuqiao County in Hebei Province is known as the native place of acrobats. It has a history of 2,000 years, and its circus has traveled around the world. Do not be surprised if you see someone somersault on the streets of Wuqiao, for they say proudly, "Grey beard and toddler as well, everyone is some kind of acrobat in Wuqiao."

The Chinese have always loved acrobatics. They are indispensable to various occasions of entertainment, from the annual Spring Festival Evening Party broadcast by the CCTV to temple fairs where all kinds of folk arts are presented. Acrobatic troupes, sometimes comprising dozens of people and sometimes just one man, perform everywhere—at theaters, on squares, in restaurants, and on streets, bringing amazement and laughter wherever they go.

Just like the Chinese character, Chinese acrobatics are featured by flexibility and steadiness, rather than novelty and dangerousness. For example, acrobats introduced the human pyramid, a traditional folk game and various stunts such as handstands, putting chair on top of chair, holding a candlestick in the mouth and juggling diabolo (*kongzhu*), which requires years of practice and the subtle use of body strength. Ropewalking is the ultimate skill. It represents the perfect unity of opposites such as movement and stability, and danger and safety. The spectators hold their breath watching the acrobat, who is immune to the excitement below, like a monk in a trance. *Dengji* (juggling with the feet), a unique skill in Chinese acrobatics, is usually performed by female acrobats. The things that can be juggled are varied—from a silk umbrella to a wooden table, from a round wine jar to a long ladder—even a humans can be juggled and spun so fast that the audience sees only a blur of figures. As an art rooted in daily life, acrobatics use domestic utensils such as bowls, plates, jars and ropes. For example, in *zhuandie*

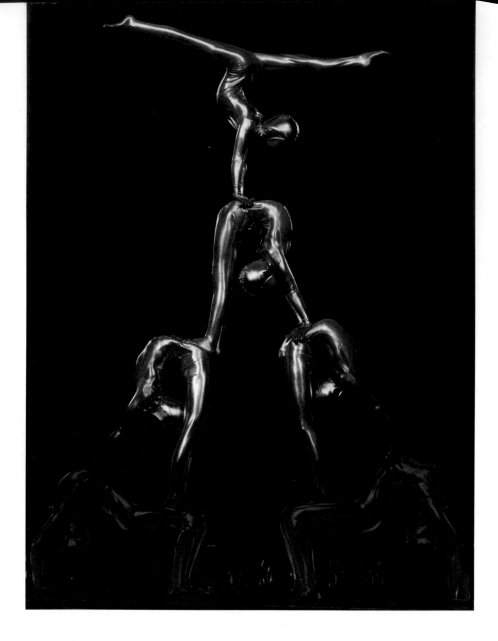

Women's ju-titsu.

(spinning plates), the acrobat spins plates on poles up to one-meter long, like lotus leaves fluttering in the wind.

Acrobats are respected in China. Learning the skill at a very young age, they endure years of training to become professionals. As the old saying goes, "a minute of performance is worth ten years of practice." Those who are in this occupation think highly of the masters and cherish the skills so that the heritage can be handed down from generation to generation.

Flying Kites

The Chinese began to make and fly kites 2,000 years ago. They are called "yao" (sparrow hawk) in the south and "yuan" (glede) in the north. The homophone of yaoyuan in Chinese means far away, and nobody is sure if it is just a coincidence or a metaphor.

Kites were originally used for military reasons. Historical records show that General Hanxin in the Han Dynasty flew kites to measure the distance between his camp and the Palace Weiyang, which he planned to occupy. Emperor Wudi in the Liang Dynasty used kites to send messages asking for reinforcement. By the Five Dynasties (907–960) palace maids fixed bamboo strips on kites, which flew in the wind (*feng*) with a sound like that of a zither (*zheng*), and a kite has since been called *fengzheng* in China. After the Song and Yuan dynasties (960–1368), kites flew out of the imperial palace into the realm of the common people and became very popular

A craftsman is making kites.

A traditional hard-winged kite flying
in the sky.

Children flying a kite
after school.

during the Ming and Qing dynasties (1368–1911).
Six children flying kites are depicted in a simple and
adorable way in the famous picture scroll *Along the River
during Pure Brightness Day* , known to be an encyclopedia
of ancient Chinese social life. Cao Xueqin, author of the
classical novel *A Dream of Red Mansions*, was a kite fan,
too, and personally recorded 43 ways of kite-making.

Spring is the best season for flying kites. In early April,
around Pure Brightness Festival (Tomb-Sweeping Day),
it is warm with a moderate east wind. People go for a
walk in the countryside and fly all kinds of kites. Some
cut the thread holding the kites when they are flying
high, hoping that misfortune will disappear with them.
Although this is only a wish, kite-flying does help to keep
the doctor away. Who can deny it is a healthy activity
running around and stretching the body in the sunshine?

There are different types and styles of kites. Kite
cultures vary a great deal, too. Beijing natives like to
fly *shayan* (sandy swallow). Those drawn with black

ink are called *heiguodi* (the black bottom of a pot), which look similar to the facial makeup in traditional operas. Tianjiners are good at making soft-winged kites in the shape of insects or birds. Sometimes they put together many small ones to make a big kite. The famous *longtouwugong* (centipede with dragon's head) made in Yangjiang, Guangdong Province can be up to 100 meters long. Equipped with several or even dozens of whistles, *shaokoubanyao* (whistling sparrow hawk) of Nantong, Jiangsu Province flies with a deafening sound that reminds you of waves breaking upon the seashore. The best kites are made in Weifang, Shandong Province, known as "the kite capital." The International Kite Festival held there each year draws people from all over the world, making the Chinese *yao* and *yuan* fly to faraway lands.

Stands selling kites are available almost everywhere in Weifang, Shandong Province.

Folk Sports

The Chinese care about the health of their body as well as their mind. Sport is not only undertaken by professionals in grand competitions but also by ordinary men and women for daily recreation. For example, in *bahe* (tug of war), two teams pull at opposite ends of a rope until one team drags the other over a line on the ground. To win, a unified effort is perhaps more important than individual strength.

Tiaosheng (rope skipping) is a yard game popular in the Tang Dynasty. With just a rope, people have invented many ways to play and compete. You can skip by yourself or with another person; sometimes, two people swing a rope, while a team skips one by one. Moreover, you can jump on one foot, two feet or hop from one foot to another. Those with better skills can turn the rope two or three times in a single jump. Group rope skipping is very common. When the long rope is swung with cracks, the first person begins to skip before others joining one by one, and the air buzzes with excitement. Some extremely skillful skipper can turn around freely or bend their knees to touch the ground while skipping.

Some school children are skipping a rope on the playground during a class break.

Another popular activity is spinning tops, one of the ancient toys of the Chinese. With one end tapered to a point, it seems unable to stand. But if you twine a piece of string around it and throw it out, it will spin on the ground. You can whip it when it slows down, making it continue its "dance."

Children in the countryside often make their own tops and compete against each other. The one with the top that spins the longest and steadiest will become the "chief," respected by every other child. Some skillful children can make their top spin for minutes at one go.

Aged people are enjoying playing diabolos in a park.

A bamboo toy that developed from the top, *kongzhu* (diabolo), has axis, wheels and openings on the side to make it whistle when spinning. While tops are whipped, diabolos must be "juggled." A good player can make it dance vigorously on a piece of rope just like a violinist handling his bow. Practice makes perfect. It takes correct posture and the subtle use of one's strength to play with the diabolo. Only those who are sensitive, dexterous, brave and careful can become good players. It is also a classic in traditional acrobatics. A master can do things as small as a lid of a teacup and as big as a round table-board. As for the amateurs, diabolo is just a fun sport. In north China, its crystal-clear and melodious whistling can often be heard in winter and spring.

Shuttlecock (also known as featherball) is another popular sport in China. Besides a feather, the top can also

People are kicking the shuttlecocks near Tiantan Park.

be made from paper, cloth and plastic. There are usually four ways of kicking a shuttlecock, with the basic one called *pan* (kicking with the inner inside of your ankle), and the other three *guai* (kicking with the outer side of your ankle), *ke* (kicking with your knees) and *beng* (kicking with the tip of your foot). Shuttlecocks can be kicked alone, with one other or with several people. It does not matter how it's kicked as long as it's airborne. It is a good exercise, as players have to be quick of eye and deft of foot.

Mysteries and Wonders in Traditional Chinese Puzzles

The Chinese have always been concerned about the all-round development of man. Confucianism emphasizes the six classical arts of rites, music, archery, riding, writing and arithmetic, which cover almost every discipline and skill. As exercise for the mind, traditional Chinese puzzles are not only entertaining but also educational.

Huarong path, together with the magic tube invented by the Hungarians and the diamond chess from France,

The story of *Huarong* Path–General Guan Yu lets Cao Cao escape.

School children are playing the seven-piece puzzle.

are praised as the three incredible examples of puzzles. It is based on a chapter in Romance of the Three Kingdoms, a famous novel about the competition for power among the three kingdoms led by Liu Bei, Sun Quan and Cao Cao respectively. Huarong path is where General Guanyu, brother of Liu, out of loyal gratitude, deliberately lets Cao, who had been defeated by the allied forces of Liu and Sun, escape. The puzzle Huarong path is a rectangular board with 10 pieces, including the biggest one (Cao Cao), five generals half his size, and four soldiers one unit smaller than the generals. The pieces are arranged in certain ways and only one piece can be moved every time, until Cao moves to the exit and escapes. With several hundred possible ways of arrangement, this puzzle has engrossed mathematicians the world over.

Qiqiaoban (literally seven boards of cunning), a square cut into seven pieces to be reassembled into over 1,600 different figures, has become popular in China ever since the Ming and Qing dynasties. Also known as Tangram, it is a puzzle that fascinates the world. Napoleon reportedly played it to pass the time during his days of exile.

Legend has it that the luban lock was invented by the famous artisan Gongsun Ban of the state of Lu in the Spring and Autumn Period (770–476 BC). It is composed of six pieces of wood with notches. Without one nail or one cord, these pieces fit together perfectly. Ancient Chinese architecture is featured by such structures, with the girders, pillars, purlins and rafts all joined ingeniously by the notches.

Popular from the Song Dynasty, the Chinese ring puzzle is composed of nine rings and a handle (sword). The challenge is to remove the rings from the handle and put them back again. It tests skills of mathematics and spatial ability. You can also make figures like a floral basket and palace lantern with the rings.

Other puzzles like *gongdaobei* (the fair cup), *yinshuiniao* (drinking bird), *lubanqiu* (Luban Ball), *sixiren* (figure celebrating four happy occasions), gobang and nine-lattice puzzle are all fantastic mind exercises. The Chinese is an old nation but is young at heart. Having proved its ingenuity with the four great inventions (paper-making, compass, gunpowder and movable type), the accurate pi and the magnificent works like the Great Wall, everyday Chinese lives are also full of excitement. For them, the ultimate purpose of life is to be happy, and they seem to know the secret of happiness.

Various Folk Customs on the Temple Fairs

The worship of gods and Buddha occupied a significant part in people's lives in the past. Pious men and women gathered in temples to pray for blessings, which brought prosperity to people such as peddlers and folk entertainers. Then came *miaohui* (temple fairs), which amazingly combine religious rituals, markets, entertainment, folk arts and social activities. Held every Spring Festival in temples, at parks, on streets and in the countryside, temple fairs provide a stage for various forms of folk culture.

Everything can be sold at temple fairs, from plants and birds to antiques and paintings; there are clothes and shoes, pots and pans, needles and threads and even grain crops. You can also see china, tinwork, cloisonné and enamel. Kites, lanterns, windmills, silk pouches in various shapes and colors are dazzling. Papercuttings in particular have a ready market during Spring Festival.

A folk artist is performing changing various facial expressions rapidly and spitting fire.

Everybody "invites" (they don't call it "buy") pieces in the shape of "福" (happiness) and "寿" (longevity). Other popular designs include "吉庆有余" (luck and affluence) and "吉祥如意" (luck as one wishes). The craftsmen sell what they are making right at the fairs. They blow sugar figurines, knead soft clay into art ware, make dolls with the husk of coconuts, and weave crickets, dragonflies and little baskets for katydids with straws. You can also find shadow-play figures hand-made from high-quality leather and painted in red, yellow, cyan, green and black. These relics provide a glimpse of a dying art form. You can also taste all kinds of food with local flavor, such as noodles and barbeque from the north, and dim sum and soup from the south. Folk artists set up stalls, providing traditional operas, acrobatics, magic, martial arts, songs, dances and other live entertainment.

The Chinese like to celebrate traditional festivals in *hui* (large gatherings). Besides *miaohui* (temple fairs), there are also *fengzhenghui* (kite fairs), *saimahui* (horse races), *longzhouhui* (dragon boat races), *duigehui* (people singing back and forth) and *Nadamn* games (Mongolian festival of harvest). *Shehuo* plays, held on the 15th of the first lunar month, is a parade of land boats, stilt-walking, lion dances and other stunts, led and directed by a traditional orchestra. *Shanhui* (mountain fairs), held twice a year in Jinan on the third day of the third lunar month and the ninth day of the ninth lunar month, is an occasion for Buddha worship and outings in the countryside. Stalls selling incense and all kinds of local products are set up along the road in Mountain Qianfo (a-thousand-buddhas). Guang Zhou hosts flower fairs every Lunar New Year's Eve, when the streets are lit up, with peonies, lilies, chrysanthemum, dahlia and roses vying for beauty. The annual lantern festival in the Confucius temple in Nanjing is another famous event, where visitors can enjoy the great theme lanterns such as "the capital of six ancient dynasties." It is an unforgettable experience to take a boat trip down the River Qinhuai, with lavish lantern displays along the banks.

The New Era of Entertainment

Now the time has passed into the 21st century and the Chinese people have turned to a totally new way of relaxation and entertainment. More and more Chinese people have subscribed to the idea of "Life First" and have plunged with great enthusiasm into their pursuit of happiness.

With the sudden rise of the media industry, the media-based entertainment life has taken up most of Chinese people's leisure time. Since the 1980s, the popularization of television has completely changed the night life of Chinese families. Today, television is as common and necessary as pots and pans to a Chinese family. Multitudes of TV channels, varied programs, timely information, and large quantities of TV series programs have provided numerous topics for leisure talk, presented before our eyes the dazzling idols and ushered in a new era of nationwide entertainment drive.

Before long, the television culture flooded in, sparking

People are dazed by varieties of entertainment show-contest activities which have become increasingly popular in recent years.

the sluggish business of the movie industry. With the Chinese movie industry coming around to its 100th anniversary, the cinema age to which a whole generation was attached has made a quiet comeback. Cinema today is more like a kingdom of fairy tales or a magic school: the high definition pictures, the high quality sound effect, the immersing and heart-pounding images, the soul-touching artistic experience—none of these can be provided by a TV set. At the same time, the Chinese movie as the supreme form of sound and visual art in China has successfully reached the culmination of the world movie via the monitors of the fifth- and sixth-generation Chinese directors.

Although having been popularizing in China for just a decade, the Internet has exerted an earthshaking influence on the ways of relaxation and entertainment of the Chinese people. Nowadays, the so-called "post-1980s" generation that leads the fashion trend cannot do without the Internet for even a single day. This is a generation that grows up along with the Internet. These people browse information, send and receive mails, chat, do shopping, read and play games via the Internet. It is also through the Internet that they have come to know

Internet cafés are the major places of entertainment for young people.

the world and other people. They have their virtual IDs besides their real IDs. They have their cyber language besides their everyday language. Moreover, with the surge in the number of personal blogs in recent years, the netizens have more right of speech, creating a generation of "New Cyber Beings" who have the courage to think independently and express themselves freely.

Along with the rapid growth of the media industry, the tourist industry has also flourished. Traveling has been the main means of entertainment for the Chinese people. Yet the present-day travel lovers are no longer interested in the well-known scenic spots, the fixed and immutable traveling routes, or a transient glance at the landscape. The self-service travel of the backpackers, the self-driving travel of car owners, the "returning to nature" rural travel and the horizon-broadening outbound travel—all these kinds of travel have become the new favorites of tourists.

The Hong Kong Disneyland is crowded with visitors.

Cultivating Health in Accordance with the Variations of the Natural World

Integration of man and nature, an idea reflecting the spirit of classic Chinese philosophy and permeating the daily lives of Chinese people, is the theoretical basis of traditional cultivation of health.

According to the traditional theory of health cultivation, both man and nature are composed of *Qi* which is a concept in classic Chinese philosophy. Man lives on earth and under heaven and is integrated with the natural world, that is, in traditional Chinese philosophy man and nature are interrelated. Thus, the changes in the natural world will inevitably affect the physiological functions and pathological changes of the human body. The idea that man and nature are integrated

The work for the year is best begun in the spring.

with each other demonstrates the harmony and unity between them. The energy in the earth and heaven emerges in spring, increases in summer, astringes in autumn and hibernates in winter. That is why the theory of health cultivation holds that care should be taken "to invigorate Yang in spring and summer while to nourish Yin in autumn and winter." The concept of *Yangqi* refers to the energy that promotes development while the concept of *Yinqi* refers to the energy that is responsible for storage and accumulation. That is why in the traditional theory of health cultivation great attention is paid to mental cultivation, diet and activity in accordance with changes of weather in different seasons.

Spring is a season marked by renewal and the emergence of *Yangqi*. So in spring, people should go to sleep late and get up early so as to follow the fluctuation of *Yangqi*. Since spring is the season of resuscitation, people should not stay at home as they do in winter to avoid the cold. Instead, they should engage in more outdoor activities. Morning is the period marked by early augmentation of *Yangqi*, so in the morning, people should do morning exercises to absorb vital energy from nature. In spring, people should take food acrid and sweet in taste and warm in nature, avoiding cold, uncooked, sour and wrinkled foods. Generally, wheat, jujubes, oranges and peanuts are recommended; carrots, persimmons and peppers are the vegetables good for health. In spring, it is advisable to drink scented tea, which can disperse the cold that has accumulated in the body during the winter, and refresh the mind and invigorate the brain, effective for banishing lethargy.

Summer is the season marked by the prosperity and superabundance of *Yangqi*. In this season, people should go to sleep late and get up early in order to preserve *Yangqi*. During this season, fire in the human body is exuberant while lung *Qi* is deficient. That is why people cannot sleep soundly during the night. In this case, a nap in the afternoon is good for revitalizing the body. In summer, people should take food good for promoting

Qi and producing body fluid as well as clearing away heat, such as mung bean and polished, round-grain, non-glutinous rice. In summer, green tea is effective in relieving summer heat, removing toxic materials and easing thirst because it is cool in nature. In traditional Chinese medicine, diseases that occur in winter are often treated in summer. The diseases that tend to occur in winter are frequently cold and deficiency ones. In summer, *Yangqi* in the human body is superabundant, so this will be helpful for removing cold and eliminating both the primary and secondary causes of diseases. For example, respiratory system diseases, arthritis, rheumatism and chronic stomach disorders all can be effectively treated in summer with external applications, acupuncture, moxibustion and decoction. Thirty to forty days after summer solstice (June 21 or 22) are the hottest days in the year, the best period for external application.

Autumn is marked by coolness, the decline of *Yangqi* and the growth of *Yinqi*. During this season, people should go to sleep early and get up early to avoid

Seasonal changes need to be taken into consideration when taking food. Different food should be taken in different seasons.

excessive coolness. In autumn, rain often brings forth coldness. However, it is unnecessary to wear more clothes. Exposure to cold is good for stimulating body resistance against the cold in winter. Autumn is also marked by dryness, so people should avoid taking acrid foods and vegetables such as scallions, ginger, garlic and peppers. The recommended foods are sesame, polished glutinous rice, honey and milk products. The tea to be drunk in autumn is oolong tea, which is neither cold nor hot, and effective both for removing latent heat in summer and nourishing the lungs in producing fluid.

In winter, it is icy cold and the land is frozen. This season is marked by recession of *Yangqi* and predominance of *Yinqi*. Traditionally in China, people try to replenish themselves in winter by eating mutton, which is hot in nature. The vegetables recommended are lotus and edible fungus. Black tea is best to drink in winter because it is sweet and warm, helps the digestion, warms the stomach, replenishes *Qi* and strengthens the body. Winter is the season for cultivating essence, so it is advisable to go to sleep early and get up late so as to maintain essence, *Qi* and spirit inside the body.

The changes in the natural world are manifested as variations of the four seasons and the changes of elements. Since human beings are living between the earth and the heavens, they have to restrict their activities within the changes of the natural world. The sages in ancient times cultivated their health in accordance with the changes of weather in the four seasons, carefully adjusting their emotions and living conditions, regulating *Yin* and *Yang* as well as balancing various factors concerning their lives.

Cultivating Health with Traditional Chinese Medicine

The concept of cultivating health permeates all aspects of Chinese life—from daily activity to diet and adjustment of emotions, from trivial activities like combing hair and cleaning teeth to calming the mind—and generally follows the principle of maintaining balance and harmony in every aspect. When falling ill, the Chinese resort to traditional therapeutic methods.

Traditional Chinese medicine is both a science of medicine and a system of philosophy. According to traditional Chinese medicine, every human being is a small universe and the human body is an integrated whole. The inner integration of the human body is achieved by unity of the internal organs as well as the essence, *Qi* and spirit. Besides, the human body is also integrated with the external world. So in dealing with a certain disease, doctors must diagnose and treat it according to the time, season, local characteristics and customs. That is what unity between man and nature means in classic Chinese philosophy. In ancient times, science and philosophy were often commingled. That is why traditional Chinese medicine adopted the concepts of *Qi, Yin, Yang* and five elements from classic Chinese philosophy, and thereby developed a unique way of thinking.

The traditional methods used in diagnosing diseases in traditional Chinese medicine are *Wang* (inspection), *Wen* (smelling and listening), *Wen* (interrogation and inquiry) and *Qie* (taking pulse and palpation). It is said that these unique diagnostic methods were developed by Bian Que, who lived during the Warring States period (478–21BC). *Wang* (inspection) means observing the physical build, facial expression and tongue coating. Generally, obese people are often characterized by excessive phlegm, while thin people by excessive heat; quiet people are vulnerable to colds, while active people are susceptible to overabundant heat. In terms of facial expression, a whitish complexion indicates cold, a yellow complexion indicates dampness, a blue complexion indicates stagnation and a reddish complexion indicates heat. In terms of tongue coating, a thin coating indicates mild disease and a thick coating indicates severe disease. *Wen* (listening and smelling) means diagnoses diseases by smelling the breath of the patient and listening to the voice. *Wen* (interrogation and inquiry) means asking the patient or patient's relative about the major symptoms: the duration, any changes of the disease, case history and family history. This method is also used in Western medicine. *Qie* (taking pulse and palpation) is used to

A practitioner of traditional Chinese medicine is feeling the pulse of a patient.

diagnose diseases by feeling the pulse and palpating the hands, abdomen and limbs. The changes of pulse are quite significant in diagnosis. Skillful doctors can decide the nature and location of a disease simply by feeling the pulse.

Medicinal herbs are various in kind.

Traditional Chinese medicine usually uses Chinese medicinal herbs to treat diseases. These herbs are characterized by cold, hot, warm and cool properties as well as acrid, sweet, sour, bitter and salty tastes. Usually several herbs are used together to treat diseases. The forms of Chinese herbal medicine include decoction, powder, pill, tablet, granule and paste. Now, people prefer the tablets and granules of Chinese herbal medicine. In terms of therapeutic effect, decoction is the best form of medicine because it is easy to absorb. When herbs are selected and mixed together to treat a certain disease according to the theory of Chinese medicine, they are rinsed in water or millet wine or mixed, half of each. Then they are put into a earthenware pot to heat

Medicinal herbs made up according to a prescription are first decocted before being taken.

on high or low heat according to the nature of the herbs prescribed. The residue is removed and the remaining liquid is taken for therapeutic purposes. Most decoction tastes bitter but is effective for curing diseases and strengthening the body. When taking Chinese herbal medicine, the patient has to avoid certain kinds of food. For instance, in taking herbs to quell a cough, the patient should avoid eating fish; in taking herbs to subdue swelling, the patient should avoid beans; in taking herbs to induce sweating, the patient should avoid eating cold and uncooked foods; in taking herbs to stop diarrhea, the patient should avoid fruits and watermelon. Traditionally Chinese people throw the residue of decoction over the crossroads, hoping the germs are dispersed by being constantly trod upon.

Practice of Medicine at Home

To Westerners, traditional Chinese medicine is mysterious and hard to fathom. However, to the Chinese people, it is very simple and concrete: a needle, a glass, a spoon and even two palms can be used to treat diseases. In China, few people wield a scalpel, but almost every family has stored some needles, glass jars and scrapers to practice acupuncture, moxibustion, massage, cupping and scraping therapies.

Both acupuncture and moxibustion are external therapeutic methods. The points for inserting needles are called acupoints in traditional Chinese medicine. These acupoints reflect the condition of diseases and can be used to treat diseases. When an accurate diagnosis is made, doctors may insert the needle quickly into the selected acupoints and manipulate the needle with various techniques to stimulate the acupoints. Usually the patient will not feel pain when the needles are inserted into the acupoints and it rarely results in bleeding. In moxibustion, the selected moxa roll is lit and used to fumigate the surface of the body, promoting circulation of

A practitioner of traditional Chinese medicine is treating a young boy through acupuncture.

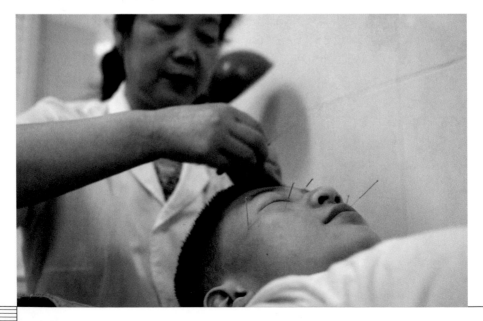

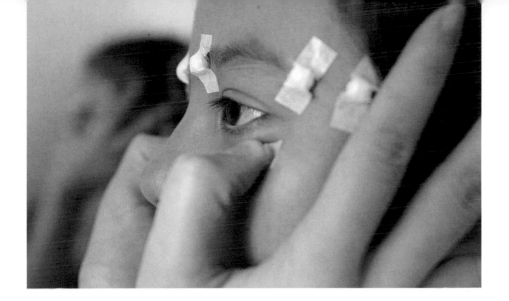

Acupoint-massage can help cure near-sightedness.

Qi and blood and adjusting the physiological functions of the body as well as preventing and treating diseases.

Tuina (massage), another therapeutic method in traditional Chinese medicine, can alleviate pain, repair injury, adjust circulation and promote rehabilitation. It is a true natural treatment because it does not use any medicinal substance. The techniques for *Tuina* are varied; some are performed with fingers, others with palms and still others with elbows or even feet. The way of treading on the body of the patient appears harsh to bystanders, but is effective for curing certain diseases without injuring the patient. Under normal conditions, *Tuina* performed for the purpose of healthcare does not need special skills and can be done in any place, at any time and by any person. Usually simple and gentle kneading and rubbing can relieve fatigue and calm the mind.

Cupping is performed with cups with the oxygen burnt, with cups boiled in water or in decoction. The first is the most common method in cupping. The cups act as a vacuum when the oxygen inside is burnt and, when attached on the surface of the body, will promote blood and *Qi* circulation, relax tendons, stimulate corresponding areas, subdue swelling, stop pain, eliminate wind and dampness. The cups used may be glass, earthenware or bamboo. Usually people just use glass cups to perform such a treatment. To perform this, just take a glass cup, place a burnt cotton ball rinsed in alcohol into the cup for a while, immediately covering the cup over the selected area. The skin drawn into the cup will gradually turn red and purple. After about 10 minutes, the cup can be removed. The cup also can be repeatedly covered over the surface of the body and then removed immediately. This is known as flashing cupping. The cup also can be pushed back and forth over the surface of the body. This is known as mobile cupping. When the cup is removed, a round seal will be left over the surface of the body, a sign of the therapeutic effect.

Cupping is usually done on the smooth and thick muscle of the body. The traditional method of cupping is to turn the cups vacuum by burning ethyl alcohol in the cups to have the oxygen burnt out.

Scraping therapy is performed with a horn of an ox. When performing such a treatment, the practitioner applies oil on the skin and then scrapes up and down and from the central region to the lateral region till the skin appears purple. This method is usually done in summer and autumn to deal with skin problems caused by invasion of wind, cold, summer heat, dryness and fire into the body. This treatment can remove pathogenic factors from the internal organs, invigorate blood to eliminate stagnation, clear away heat to remove toxins and promote metabolism in the body. Such a treatment is as effective as other therapeutic methods like acupuncture, *Tuina* and cupping. It is a sort of acupuncture treatment without needles, *Tuina* without using hands and cupping without using any cups. Folk practice of scraping therapy is very simple; sometimes a cup of water and a spoon are enough to perform such a treatment. In the rural areas, old peasants still use scraping therapy to treat common colds caused by wind and heat. The therapeutic effect is quite significant. If you see brown and purple skin around someone's shoulder area, you need not be surprised. It is not scarring, just signs of the scraping treatment. Usually three days after treatment, the patient will feel as energetic as usual.

Exercises for Externally Training the Muscles and Bones While Internally Cultivating *Qi*

Today globalization is a worldwide trend. With such a development, quite a number of English words have been adopted into Chinese language, such as sofa, coffee and jeep. However, the English language has also adopted some Chinese concepts; Kung Fu is one example. Kung Fu is an exercise composed of the elements of traditional Chinese military skills, training arts and physical and mental cultivation. In a narrow sense, training arts refer to what is known as martial arts in the West, including various schools of art, such as Shaolin, Wudang, Emei, Nanquan, Xingyi, Taiji and Bagua, etc. Military skills are often related to traditional weapons, such knife, arms and sword. And physical and mental cultivation concentrates on directing *Qi* to flow all through the body by means relaxation of the mind.

The movies starred by Li Xiaolong contributed greatly to the dissemination of Chinese Kung Fu to the whole world.

Li Xiaolong and Jin Yong contributed greatly to the dissemination of Kung Fu to the world. Thanks to films, the Kung Fu developed by Li Xiaolong is very popular in the Western world. Jin Yong has written many novels about Kung Fu. His novels are full of the traditional cultural elegance and Chinese spirit. Li practiced Kung Fu while Jin writes about Kung Fu. Both of them contributed a great deal to the development of Kung Fu all over the world.

"All the Kung Fu under the heaven can find their origin from Shaolin Monastery." Shaolin Monastery in Songshan Mountain of Henan Province, renowned at home and abroad, is the cradle of Shaolin school of martial arts.

Traditional Chinese Kung Fu concentrates on training both the external and internal body, known as the internal school and external school as represented by Shaolin and Wudang, both of which are the representatives of Chinese Kung Fu. The martial art represented by the Shaolin school is marked by sturdiness, pose, resistance and human sense while the Kung Fu represented by Wudang school is characterized by gentleness, mental direction,

A martial arts monk from Shaolin Monastery is practicing martial arts.

body cultivation and stillness.

The internal school of Kung Fu concentrates on cultivating *Qi*. This way of practice is known as *Qigong*, which is marked by self-regulation through mental direction, respiration and pose adjustment as well as regulation of the mind, breath and physical activity so as to invigorate the potential energy in the body, balance the psychological aspects and strengthen the body. *Qigong* is the supreme stage of health cultivation and can only be managed by a few masters.

Qigong is a magic exercise and is not easy to practice. So today in China the most commonly practiced exercise is *Taijiquan* which was developed about 300 years ago. Though there are various schools of *Taijiquan*, the essentials are the same, that is, mental concentration, spiritual relaxation, gentle action and continuous performance. This exercise is often practiced by middle-

Upper: The Taoist abbot of the Wudang Mountain is imparting the art of *Taiji* sword to his followers.

Lower: As part of the quintessence of Chinese culture, *Taijiquan* has captivated many enthusiasts from all over the world with its charm.

aged and old people. Early in the morning in parks, you can find many people practice this exercise together. After a while of practice, they feel quite refreshed, enjoying mental peace and physical relaxation.

Nowadays, martial arts masters are hard to come by, but the concept that "Life depends on doing exercises" has taken roots in the hearts of people. Considered as the contemporary "Kung Fu" (martial arts) by the Chinese people, doing exercises and fitness training at present have become the essential ways the Chinese people are currently practicing for keeping fit both in body and mind.

Playing football and basketball, which is all the rage throughout the world, is also extremely popular among the Chinese people. There is no lack of spare-time master players of football and basketball among young people, particularly among college students. Our national ball, table tennis ball, and badminton, which is easy to learn and play, boast a massive of players in China. People often play table tennis ball and badminton in early morning, at dusk or during noon breaks. Though it has not been a long time since the sports events like billiards,

Skiing fans are enjoying the fun of skiing to their hearts' content.

In a gymnasium, a coach is earnestly guiding her trainee in a fitness-training.

tennis and squash were first introduced to China, they immediately became popular among office workers. The ancient people often wrote about mountains and rivers to express their feelings, whereas the sports events the contemporary Chinese people are going in for at present are also closely linked with mountains and rivers. Mountain-climbing and swimming, two outdoor exercises suitable both for the old and the young, can be either athletics sports or entertainment activities, either fashionable or traditional exercises. Moreover, outdoor exercises like rock-climbing, skiing, diving, windsurfing, automobile race, extreme sports popular mainly among the younger generation and team events which focus on team spirit make up all the entirely new parts of the fashion sports in China.

In comparison with athletic sports, fitness training is the way of keeping fit that is closer to everyday life. Nowadays, varieties of professional gymnasiums, fitness centers and body-building clubs are nothing new in big and mid-size cities in China. Going to fitness centers has almost become the third most important spare-time activity in which the urban white-collar employees are interested, ranking right after shopping and

Jogging on a jogging machine, an urban white-collar employee is dripping with sweat.

entertainment. In fitness centers, men would prefer to do physical exercises through sports apparatuses, while women are deeply interested in specialized training courses. Men keep fit through body-building, while women pursue beauty through fitness training. Practicing Oriental yoga can not only help to improve one's health, but also help to cultivate one's mind or moral character. Practicing Western Pilates can not only help one to keep fit, but also help to better one's build. Calisthenics is dynamic and full of vigor. Ballet sends forth graceful charm. Overflowing with enthusiasm, Latin dance and belly dance transmit the cultures and customs of South America and the Middle East respectively. Moreover, with the implementation of the "Nationwide Body-building Project," body-building activities have become popular in most urban communities, and even have reached ordinary households in China. The sports and body-building apparatuses installed within the communities have made it possible for the aged and the children to have the chance to do physical training right in front of their houses. In addition, household sports apparatuses have also helped to turn households into "domestic gymnasiums." The Chinese people shall never call a halt to the pursuit of a healthier life.

Food for Health Cultivation

Traditionally Chinese people believe that food and medicine share the same origin. It is said that decoction was developed by Yin Yi in the Shang Dynasty (1600–1046 BC) when he was cooking food. This concept also indicates that food can be used as medicine and medicine can be added to food. Such an idea accounts for the development of diet therapy.

Diet therapy means choosing certain foods to regulate the functions of the body for therapeutic purposes. Grains, meat, fruit and vegetables, just as with medicinal herbs, also possess cold, hot, warm and cool properties. For instance, barley, mutton, lychee and Chinese chives are warm and hot in property; millet, duck, persimmons and wax gourd are cold and cool in property; and polished glutinous rice, pork, apple and sweet potato are mild in property. Traditional Chinese medicine treats diseases with the principle "that hot diseases should be treated with herbs cold in property while cold diseases should be treated with herbs hot in property." Based on such a principle, people with warm constitutions should take foods cold and cool in property while people with

The Chinese people who believe that food and medicine share the same origin prefer tonic food.

Left: Tendril-leaved fritillary bulb and pears, the best tonic fruits in the autumn season, have the effect of moistening the lungs and reducing phlegm.

Right: Both pleasant to the eye and delicious, steamed bread made of corn is a kind of healthy food deeply loved by ordinary Chinese people.

cold and cool constitutions should take foods warm in property. Foods not only can provide energy for maintaining life, but also can affect results for curing certain diseases. Drugs bear toxic effects. However, if one takes foods as medicine, there will be no toxic effect. Of course different foods bear different effects and may be fit for different people. Generally, foods with the same property and taste can work together to greater effect. For instance, the lily and pear can be taken together for the purpose of clearing away heat from the lungs and moistening the lungs; ginger decoction and black sugar can be taken together for the purpose of warming the body and dispersing cold. Sometimes different kinds of foods may restrict each other. For instance, ginger can prevent fish from causing skin rash and turnips can reduce the effect of Chinese yam in nourishing Qi. There are still some kinds of foods that should never be taken together; otherwise, serious problems will occur. For instance, when crab and persimmons are taken together, diarrhea will result; when beet and chestnuts are taken together, vomiting will happen; when pork and river snail are taken together, the intestines and stomach will be damaged; and when shrimp and jujubes are taken together, poisoning will be the result.

Today food therapy is becoming simpler. People just use raw food (for example, maize, sorghum, different millet, various beans, etc., as distinct from wheat flour and rice) as their diet. Raw food is not processed, so the natural elements are preserved. Modern research indicates that raw food contains more vitamin, minerals and edible fibers which are good in resisting cancer, lowering blood pressure, protecting the brain, cleaning the intestines and

nourishing
the skin. With the rapid development of
the economy in China, today people prefer
raw food to delicacies from the land and sea.
The food diet is beneficial to the health to some
extent. However, it cannot wholly replace medicine.
Chinese medicinal herbs not only can be processed
into decoction, tablets, pills, granules and powder, but
also can be added to food. That is what medicated food
means. Medicated food can serve as a supplementary
therapy, quite effective for dealing with certain kinds of
diseases, strengthening the body and preventing diseases.
The rules for compatibility of medicinal herbs with foods
were decided by people in ancient times according to
their experience, which have been and are still being
followed today. For instance, pork can be cooked
together with *Huang Lian* (Coptis Chinensis, the rhizome
of Chinese goldthread) and *Cang Zhu* (Atractylodes
Chinensis, Chinese atractylodes). However, mutton
cannot be cooked with *Ban Xia* (Pinellia Ternata, the tuber
of pinellia) and *Chang Pu* (calamus), garlic cannot be
used with *Di Huang* (Rehmaannia Glutinosa, glutinous
rehmannia) and vinegar cannot be used with poria.

It is common knowledge to the Chinese people that
foods can have certain therapeutic effects on their health.
For instance, when catching cold, they will naturally take
garlic to cure it; when suffering from diarrhea, they will
drink a cup of wine to stop it; when drunk, they will take
tomato juice to neutralize the effects of alcohol; when
tired, they will eat a banana to refresh them. So you see
how Chinese people enjoy their lives: they cultivate their
health and live a happy life simply by means of adjusting
their food intake.

As the nutritional value of all kinds of food grains is currently being recognized by modern people, eating all kinds of food grains has become a new fashion.